Reinhard Hesse

What Is Philosophy About?

Reinhard Hesse

What Is Philosophy About?

Fundamental philosophical questions between truth and power

LIT

Bibliographic information published by the Deutsche Nationalbibliothek
The Deutsche Nationalbibliothek lists this publication in the Deutsche Nationalbibliografie; detailed bibliographic data are available on the Internet at http://dnb.d-nb.de.

ISBN 978-3-643-80221-7

A catalogue record for this book is available from the British Library

Klosbachstr. 107
CH-8032 Zürich
Tel. +41 (0) 44-251 75 05 Fax +41 (0) 44-251 75 06
E-Mail: zuerich@lit-verlag.ch http://www.lit-verlag.ch

Distribution:

In the UK: Global Book Marketing, e-mail: mo@centralbooks.com
In North America: International Specialized Book Services, e-mail: orders@isbs.com
In Germany: LIT Verlag Fresnostr. 2, D-48159 Münster
Tel. +49 (0) 2 51-620 32 22, Fax +49 (0) 2 51-922 60 99, e-mail: vertrieb@lit-verlag.de

In Austria: Medienlogistik Pichler-ÖBZ, e-mail: mlo@medien-logistik.at
e-books are available at www.litwebshop.de

Meinen Eltern

Content

ACKNOWLEDGMENTS

I thank my brother, Wolfgang Hesse, Bonn, for his critical reading and constructive suggestions and Benjamin Dollenmaier, student at the University of Konstanz, for his help in preparing the manuscript and for numerous useful observations. I owe special thanks to Professor Hideshi Funao of the University of Aichi, Japan, for his translation of the original manuscript into Japanese during my time there as visiting professor. It was his interest that motivated me to bring this work to completion. Thanks must also go to Claire Albrecht, visiting student from Australia at the University of Konstanz, and to my old friend Dr. Denis Jonnes, Professor at the English Department of the University of Fukuoka, Japan, who decisively improved this English version with their linguistic feeling and conceptual understanding.

PREFACE

In the following work, I have written down some of the ideas that have emerged over the years in discussions with students, young people in general and others interested in philosophy and philosophical ethics.

I have attempted to restrict the wide range of topics addressed in these discussions to those that appear most important to me, and to give systematic and historical structure to the relative disorder usually occurring in free discussions.

Young people in particular, who are still searching for their own direction in life (as well as adults who may have begun to doubt their earlier convictions) have a lively and legitimate interest in posing fundamental questions about life. Philosophy addresses such questions and attempts to offer answers. "Philosophy" in this context means not just the "scientific community" of established academic philosophers, but rather the endeavor of the self-reflective human being to discover who we as humans essentially are, how we can attain knowledge, and, not least, how we can know what we should do.

It appears to me that current academic philosophy is on the whole reluctant to adequately deal with this human interest. When it does, it mostly does so in a merely historiographical sense: Which philosophers have asked which questions, and have offered which answers? To articulate clear positions on the elementary questions of life (which may well turn out to be not so elementary after all) – saying, in effect, "this is how I see these matters, and for the following reasons" – does not seem to be *en vogue* in contemporary academic discussion.

In any case, this is *not* the approach that I have taken in the book before you. I have tried instead to identify and clarify the core questions that arose in these discussions and to answer them as clearly as possible – though certainly from my own perspective. I may have made mistakes, and may have overlooked some important aspects. It is my hope not to have erred greatly. I have no doubt, however, that I have passed over important considerations, over even a great many of these, and for this I must take responsibility. Criticism is welcome.

One omission is evident to me already: In one form or another, I should have mentioned what has been said about the role of humor; and this for a serious reason. In philosophy we take the questions and problems of life seriously, trying to "get a handle on them"; but how, if not by means of humor, can we both take these subjects seriously and at the same time distance ourselves from them? Loss, suffering, misfortune, pain and even death lose their power over us – at least for a moment – when we put them at arm's length by laughing at them.

The experienced reader will quickly recognize that my systematic ideas are inspired by the so-called transcendental-pragmatic philosophy of language and foundation of ethics, as developed in the most consistent way by Karl-Otto Apel. His writings, to which I can only refer here in a general way, are addressed to an academic audience, in particular to the small community of those with a philosophical background. This is regrettable, given that the subject matter of transcendental philosophy concerns not only a small circle of philosophical 'experts', but rather everyone. I have attempted to present the core ideas in such a way that they can be understood by every reader, and I hope on the whole to have succeeded in this.

Beyond this, I have tried to move transcendental-pragmatic philosophy into a larger context: What are its consequences for our understanding of *religion* and of *politics*; more precisely, of *political economy*?

So far, transcendental-pragmatic philosophy has dealt with these consequences either not at all or only on the periphery. In my view, the gravity of these consequences requires them to be explicitly and clearly addressed. I have tried to do so in this book. I may sometimes have erred; sometimes arguments may come across as harsh. In any case, much remains to be worked out in detail. Here, too, I hope at least to have gotten to the heart of the matter.

I have tried to write in a way that is accessible to the general public. However, the reader might sometimes feel moved to explore further into these topics. The reference books (both dictionaries and encyclopedias) which could be used for this are numerous. The following dictionaries are generally considered to be useful for beginners: "The Dictionary of Philosophy" by Dagobert D. Runes, and "The Oxford Dictionary of Philosophy".

The present book is divided into two sections; the first being predominantly systematic, the second predominantly historical. I attempted to retain some of the flavor of the open discussions upon which the book is based by maintaining a question and answer structure.

The intention is to remain as lively as possible while confronting readers with fundamental questions – questions which they can relate to their own lives and experiences.

Introduction: What is philosophy all about?

Q: What is philosophy all about?
A: It's about gaining certain fundamental insights.

Q: Which ones?
A: I think we can discern two kinds of fundamental insights: Those that are *systematic* and those that are *historical* in nature.

Q: What are the *systematic* fundamental insights?
A: First, that it is necessary to use one's own reason (Kant: "Habe Mut, dich deines eigenen Verstandes zu bedienen!" *Sapere aude*!) This is at the same time the most difficult to accomplish.
Second, that there is no other source than man's own reason to tell him what is truth, sense, good and evil.
Third, as a consequence, that we as humans are dependent on one another in our otherwise helpless search for truth and morality.
Fourth, that to be a "philosopher" means to be a *friend* of wisdom (truth) and not its possessor. I am a friend, however, only to the extent that I make an effort to be one.
Fifth, that as a consequence of this effort, insight must always be open to justifiable revision, and hence,
Sixth, that philosophical insight cannot give up its claim to validity, that is, to truth (not even in the context of postmodern relativism), nor can it flee to the supposed security of religious beliefs or other ideological dogmas. The possibility of revision only strengthens the claim to validity.
And seventh, that the simple act of posing a serious question, which necessarily is part of the *conditio humana*, as described above, implies at the same time the acknowledgement of basic principles of an ethic of virtual universalism (in the so-called performative-pragmatic sense); that therefore man cannot be man without, through the medium of language, having

implicitly acknowledged his fellow human beings and having accepted the necessity of a reciprocal relationship with equal rights and duties.

Q: And the *historical*?

A: Above all, this: the history of philosophy can be understood as a gradual unfolding of the above-mentioned insights; or perhaps better, a muddling through in order to uncover them. We can discern three basic steps along this path: Plato, Kant, and the Philosophy of Language. First, Plato, who – in my view, correctly – stresses that truth can only be found by means of argumentative dialogue, but who at the same time – in my view, incorrectly – understands this kind of dialogue as being a mere means for the rediscovery of eternal truths existing in a speculative world of ideas, itself independent from any human dialogue.

Second, Kant, who – in my view, correctly – makes the step from heteronomy to autonomy. For him, it is no longer Plato's world of ideas, the transcendent God of Christianity, nor the Empiricists' natural senses that give us orientation; rather, we must orient *ourselves*. "Habe Mut, dich deines eigenen Verstandes zu bedienen!" – Dare to use your own reason (mind)! At the same time, Kant – in my view, incorrectly – takes the operation of reason to be on the whole a solitary mental process. And finally,

Third, Philosophy of Language, which, beginning with Peirce and Wittgenstein, attempts to overcome the deficits of Kant's "Philosophy of Mind", and, in the writings of Karl-Otto Apel, derives, via transcendental-pragmatic reflection, an inescapable ethical foundation from the necessarily linguistic nature of human enquiry. To put it simply: Thinking depends on language (communication) which itself cannot exist without a minimal ethical consensus on virtually universalistic equal rights and duties.

The appeal to communicative situations in which all participants interact unimpeded as free and equal partners is by no means utopian. This is for at least two reasons, the first being that communicative situations of this kind *are* in fact (empirically) an essential basis for our everyday life – from conversations about the daily necessities of private life to debates conducted within public bodies, for example in parliaments, which in fact lead to decisions based on consensus far more often than one might think. Secondly, even though freedom and equality empirically exist at an insufficient level, one is required nevertheless to make use of these postulates as counter-factual suppositions. Even the most radical opponent cannot avoid asking serious questions – if only in a strategic sense. Even he needs secured knowledge (truth). Aside from lack of goodwill, lack of insight and of course inadequate paths of communication (in the technical sense), it is above all the exercise of power that allows the described ideal situation to *appear* utopian. But it is *not*. It is an anticipation inextricably bound to every seriously posed question.

The smaller the obstacles which stand in the way of this anticipation, the more easily we will be able to succeed, in Kant's words, in discovering *truth*, in doing the *right thing*, and in not being deceived by empty *hopes.*

The exercise of power cannot help but distort the communicative situation. The central task of political philosophy is to analyze this distortion and find ways to overcome it. Since power mostly results from economic structures, political philosophy has no choice but to concern itself also with *normative political economy*.

This is due to the fact that philosophy is essentially enlightenment, and thus is bound to the great and eternal task of overcoming power.

SYSTEMATIC PART

Q: Let us begin by boldly asking some *fundamental questions* about our existence!
First of all: Where does the *world* (the cosmos, lifeless nature) come from? In other words, why is there something and not instead nothing (as Leibniz asks)?

A: As I see it, the only honest answer is that there is no answer; moreover, that there cannot ever be one, because everything that we could say in answer would already be "of this world".

Q: And how does *life* come into the lifeless cosmos?

A: This, too, we cannot answer, because every answer would necessarily presuppose the prior existence of life.

Q: And, finally, where does man as a "rational being", with its ability to act freely, come from; more specifically, how does *freedom* enter into the (deterministic) realm of nature?

A: This, too, we unfortunately cannot answer, because every answer we might give (by using reason) would necessarily presuppose the existence of freedom.

Q: These are disappointing answers! Is "unfortunately" all that philosophy can say on these matters?

A: No: Philosophy can justify this "unfortunately" (namely in the manner suggested above, which we will shed clearer light on later) and it can show that – in another, well-understood sense – the justification of this "unfortunately" contains an "answer" (of the only sort that is possible for us as humans) to the basic questions of our existence.

Q: How so?

A: To begin with, philosophy directs attention to the fact that the use of *Where from?* in these three questions – "Where does the cosmos come from? Where does life come from? Where does reason come from?" – makes sense only in reference to a certain presupposition, namely, the *existence* of some such origin, beginning, or act of creation. We then might ask exactly *how* this presupposition can be defined (thus, the more fundamental question as to *whether* this presupposition can be held at all remains unasked.) Logically, such questions about ultimate origins rest on a *petitio principii* – one already makes use of what must first have been constructed. Concretely, the words "Where from" in the above questions are being used incorrectly in the same manner as when a child asks its parents "Where did I come from?" (Answer: "Your parents conceived you.")

Children are conceived by parents, flowers arise from seeds, tuberculosis comes from bacteria. Here the question about origins makes sense: The question "Where from?" refers to a context from which we can know that an answer is *possible* (whether the answer can really be given, is simply a matter of whether our search for it is successful or not). In other words, we use the question "Where from?" precisely in such contexts. When we are confronted with new circumstances and wish to identify the (human) reason or (natural) cause that is prior to them, we ask this question. In casually extending the use of these two words to the realm of the three above-mentioned fundamental questions of existence, we implicitly presuppose the same sort of context for which the words were initially adopted and in which their meaning is well understood (i.e., the search, under given contextual conditions, for a potential origin – a human reason or natural cause). Whether it is *at all possible* to identify such an origin is the underlying problem that we confront here. More precisely, this is our true concern. To articulate this concern, we use language (the question "Where from?") through which an answer is already implied: "Yes, in principle we can discover the origin (of the world, of life, of reason)". By transferring the words' meaning from their everyday or scientific use to the realm of our three fundamental philosophical questions, we fall into a linguistic trap.

Q: And where is the "answer" that was promised (albeit warily)?

A: Before we can speak of an "answer," we must first clarify the question. We have seen that the original question "Where does the world (and life, and reason) come from?" contains a linguistic error. The very question suggests its own answer: "Yes, it is in principle possible to recognize their ultimate origins." Yet, this assertion is not an answer. It is merely an explicit statement of the presupposition already built into the meaning of the question (through the words "Where from").

Q: How then can we ask the question better?

A: It ought to be posed in a form that makes evident the problematic assumption implicit in "Where from?", for example, by asking: *Is* there anything that is prior to the world, to life, to reason? Is there anything that would explain these 'existentialities', make them understandable for us?

Q: Does this help us?

A: At first, no. Taking the question "Is there anything...?" at face value (namely, as a request for a substantive reply) the same problem arises as when we use the question "Where from?" On this level (the so-called apophantic-propositional level), it is also a case of linguistic misuse. The question "Is there anything that is prior to the world?" is a misuse of language (i.e., does not make sense), because the word "world" (referring to "everything that exists") cannot be further reduced. One cannot ask, "Is there something apart from everything?" Apart from that which 'exists' can only be that which does not 'exist'. Hence, more precisely, the question asks, "Does something exist that does not exist?" Or, in other words, "Can one say of some 'logical entity' (a 'something') that it exists *and* that it does not exist?" Logically, this is not possible (to avoid self-contradiction). Thus, the problem is not that the question about ultimate origins cannot be answered; it is rather that it cannot be asked in the first place.

Q: Can't we look at the matter (the question) from some other angle?

A: Yes, precisely by reflecting not on what the content of the question is but rather on the fact that it is, as a question, a linguistic speech act.

Q: How does that get us any further?

A: Briefly, because no question is possible that does not already presuppose the existence of the world, life, and reason. The unquestioned acceptance of these basic facts of our existence is a trivial precondition for posing any question. The existence of the world, life and reason needs no separate 'explanation' (in the sense of a derivation from supposed origins).

It *cannot* be 'deduced' because any "deduction" must take this foundation as already given.

Since Kant, the reference to the "preconditions of possibility" has been called "transcendental". The 'answer' to the fundamental questions of existence thus lies in transcendental reflection (not on a substantive level). It lies more precisely on the level of reflection about what we are *doing* when we pose such questions (it lies on the so-called "transcendental speech-pragmatic" level). In this sense it is indirectly substantive or meaningful, with regard to the irreducibility of our 'existentialities' (world, life, reason), and it defines the limits of what at all can be asked: It is impossible to question anything prior to 'existentialities' in any meaningful way, within the limits of reason.

Q: Doesn't *religion* try to give a substantive answer to these three questions?
A: Yes. Its answer in all cases is: God is the creator (of the world, of life, of reason). "Religion" means "connection" to God (from the Latin *religere* = "connect"). From the standpoint of religion, we humans can enter into a connection with God.

Q: How?
A: Mainly via belief.

Q: If one can simply "believe", then anyone can believe anything, and it all ends in chaos, with no way of knowing which belief is the right one.
A: Yes. And since this would contradict the central concern of religion, which is to deliver secure answers to our three questions, every religion is forced to establish certain tenets of belief as "right"; that is, to establish some form of ideological canon. In this sense, the Catholic Church claims to represent the "true religion," the *religio vera*.
Which beliefs are included in this canon depends on many factors, for example,

- (possibly) reasonable insights,
- traditions of the culture in which the respective religion arose,
- persons, officials (like the Pope) or institutions that are seen as authorities (perceived as capable of making such decisions as to what belongs in the canon) and, of course,
- the willingness of the people to accept certain doctrines ("dogmas") without further foundation.

In the Christian religion such doctrines are, for example, derived from the Bible (as the word of God) and from the life of Jesus (His son). The required situation-specific interpretation and continuous adaptation of the canon is then the responsibility of the Church, as necessary mediator between God and humankind. God can also appear in the form of miracles (i.e., in the suspension of natural laws, which, in any case, are also His creation). Determining which events can be classified as miracles is again the prerogative of the Church.

Once a canon is established, those who do not adhere to it are often persecuted as 'non-believers', 'apostates', 'heretics', 'witches' etc. and even physically eliminated if necessary. In Europe alone, campaigns of persecution and terror in the name of religion have certainly, over the centuries, cost millions of lives.

Q: Do all religions have this tendency to violence?

A: Yes, by necessity, but to different degrees. This may have to do with the doctrines of each religion, their historical contexts, as well as the social, economic and political circumstances in which they arose and exist.

Q: Why "by necessity"?

A: Because, in the end, religion rests on belief rather than on knowledge gained through doubt and dialogue (which also accepts the limits of possible knowledge). The necessity arises particularly if, or when, religions believe they are justified in deriving rules of practical action from their doctrines. When conflicts arise (especially with the adherents of other religions, which is quite often the case), there is no way of resolving the conflict through argumentative dialogue for a religion that really takes itself seriously. The only remaining option is to use violence (in the name of God).

Q: But doesn't Christianity, with its basic imperative of love for one's fellow beings, have a high moral claim?

A: Yes, certainly.

Q: Then everything is for the best, after all?

A: Unfortunately not quite. Christianity indeed presents a great moral step forward by comparison with other religions; for example, Judaism, in which a tribal or folk-God cares *only* for his chosen people.

Historically, Christianity has distanced itself from Judaism (from which it emerged). It was not coincidental that Jewish priests sent the self-proclaimed 'Christ' (the "savior" for all people, Jews and non-Jews, priests and laymen) to the cross – which later gave Christianity grounds for persecution.

When looking at these origins of Christianity we can easily see that everything is not "for the best." And this because the moral imperative of love for one's fellow beings is established as a doctrine of *belief*. The idea of solidarity with other human beings (more precisely, with all human beings, or yet more precisely with all rational beings) must be justified by means other than belief, for otherwise, if taken seriously, there is no other way to its realization than by force (as has happened so often in history), since rational discussion as a means is simply not an option. The last resort will always be belief, and not rational discussion. (Finding a way out of this dilemma is the central task of practical philosophy. More on this later.)

Q: Then what is to be made of the answer given by religion?

A: For the above named reasons, the answer given by religion unfortunately is not acceptable. "Unfortunately" because it would suit our human needs well not to be thrown into a cold world without beginning and end, devoid of meaning. It would be wonderful to live in a world which, from beginning to end, has order and meaning, of which we are a part. Yet the world remains indifferent, cold and meaningless. Participation (solidarity), warmth (love for one's fellow beings) and meaning (reason) are introduced by us and us alone. Or not at all.

This is the frightfully great task from which we prefer to seek refuge in the secure warmth of religious beliefs. We would love to sit like a child on God the Father's lap, letting ourselves be protected and led by him. Unfortunately, that is not possible. Hanging onto an illusion, knowing all the while that it *is* an illusion, is a luxury that may be allowed of a child, but unfortunately not of a grown and mature adult. The questions about ultimate origins have no answers; the possibility of answering them is beyond human reason. We have no choice but to meekly accept this fact. Religion's answer, in the harmless case, is an understandable human error (or a "sigh of the oppressed creature," in Marx's words); in the not so harmless case it is a fraudulent illusion or a cynical lie. In any case, it is (extremely) dangerous whenever social or political consequences are drawn.

Q: Can one then say that there is no God?

A: One can say that we do not *know* and that the *belief* in God is rendered unacceptable when rules of practical action (values, ethics) are derived from it. When rules of action based on belief alone come into conflict with one another, rational discussion as a means of peaceably resolving the conflict is not an option. In practice, this leads to violence (war) as the only remaining means.

Q: Aren't wars of religion a thing of the past?

A: Unfortunately this not the case at all. Religious motives continue to play a large role in wars (of course, there are many other motives, not the least of which are economic in nature, and often the motives are mixed). Not without reason, nowadays there is much talk of a 'renaissance of religion'. We need only think of the propensity to violence among Islamists or American Protestant fundamentalists, most evident in the claim of the former American President G. W. Bush that *God* had ordered him to wage war against Iraq. The Shiite priests of Iran sent hundreds of thousands of young men to their death in the next war against Iraq with the promise that they would be taken as martyrs into heaven.

Q: What role does religion play under the special circumstances of the atomic age?

A: A threatening one, one that indeed endangers our very existence! The self-annihilation of humankind, made possible for the first time through the development of weapons of mass destruction (not only the atomic, but also the no less dangerous biological and chemical weapons), can be interpreted from a religious perspective not only as a *sacrifice* that we must accept in the name of religious duty but even as a doorway to the 'other world' in which we find true, eternal, heavenly life (or whatever it may be called). There are too many examples in history of how inhuman religion can be to allow ourselves the hope that no one might be found ready to take this last step. We shall see, I think, that somewhere, someone will be found willing.

Q: In what form then is belief possible?

A: At most, perhaps in the form of a (private) hope. But, strictly speaking, even that is impossible, for what purpose could this hope serve other than to seek the order, compassion and meaning that we need for life and which we evidently fail to find in the cold facts of the world? "Order", "compassion" and "meaning", however, are concepts that we cannot obtain through belief; they have to be constructed via critical, differentiating reflection. *Here*, in the critical reflection of reason, we find their roots – *this* is the way. The hope that there could be any other is futile from the start; it cannot be fulfilled. However, the hope which one places in reason is *not* empty; it *can* be fulfilled. It is the overarching task of humankind and of human history. Religious hope is the beginning of an (always potentially dangerous) path to error.

Q: All the same, there are many people who have found order, compassion and meaning in religiously founded ways of life and feel happy there. Is it not arrogant to reproach them, so to speak, for feeling unjustifiably happy?

A: A religious answer to the great existential questions (as mentioned earlier) is not available. To call this observation arrogant contributes nothing to the matter. People in certain situations or practicing certain lifestyles can be "happy", and that may be pleasant for them at the moment. Yet this does not mean that their subjective state is anything more than that – subjective. Put differently, the assertion, "Way of life X makes me (us) happy" does not have the same meaning as "Way of life X is ethical". This second assertion requires its own justification, which cannot be obtained by referring to the subjective well-being of an individual or group.

Q: And what about the proofs of God's existence?

A: There are none and there can be none.

Kant has shown why these proofs, suggested throughout history, are untenable.

In any case, even if someone were to "prove" God's existence, this proof would be of no value, for God is postulated precisely as an entity not subject to human understanding; His existence is not dependent on us and our feeble proofs. That is considered to be His essential nature. If God could be proved, He would lose this nature: He would become a provable part of this world, and could no longer be considered the primordial creator.

Over and above this, an "explanation" of the existence of the world (of life, of reason) by recourse to a divine act of creation would only push the question about ultimate origins back one step, to the question of God's origin. To avoid endless regression, we have to draw the line somewhere, by simply accepting that God has no beginning – he is indeed primordial. However, by drawing this line, we fail to give the intended answer to the question about an ultimate origin. We cannot answer it through an infinite regression, or through the arbitrary declaration that God has no beginning. This *explains* nothing. In Kant's words, one has replaced something that one cannot understand (the ultimate origin of the world, of life, of reason) with something else that is even harder to understand.

Q: How can people free themselves from religious illusions?
A: By "Enlightenment", i.e., by using their reason, and by making a communal effort to find out (work out by deliberation) who they really are as human beings and how they can give meaning and warmth to their lives.

Q: So do we have to go back to the drawing board?
A: No. Human history has experienced (at least in Europe) two distinct periods of enlightenment: First in Greece (around the fifth century BC), when human thought freed itself from ancient myths, and second in modern times (roughly the eighteenth century) when human thinking freed itself from the paternalism of Christianity. Other cultures have also had similar periods. We can and must build on these.

Q: What advantage could there be for taking on the arduous endeavor of using one's own reason (which can lead to incorrect results and even prove futile)? Would it not be far simpler to follow our natural desires or *instincts* – as animals do?
A: It may well be. But only at first glance. Looking a little closer, we can see even from banal cases that this will not work. In order to survive (i.e., simply to live through the next winter) we have to distance ourselves consciously from immediate needs, like hunger, and, instead of eating all we have, we must think ahead, putting aside rations for the time when food will be hard to find. We have no instinct that would impel us to do this; it takes reflection to recognize the necessity.

In this respect, human beings are much different from animals, who can survive because their genetic coding provides any necessary behavior. Ants, for example, build their mounds in such a way that they will survive the cold winter, but they do not deliberate over it. Nor is this genetic coding the product of reflection undertaken by ants over the course of their evolution. Rather, they would not have been able to survive without the inherent support of this genetic coding. Nature brings forth an endless number of genetic patterns, of which only very few prove to be capable of enduring. Darwin called this process "survival of the fittest".

By contrast, human beings are not endowed with instincts in the same way, nor to a similar extent, that would allow them to secure their survival "blindly". They are forced to compensate for this partial lack of instinctual direction by relying on thought and deliberation.

Certainly, some animal species must do this too, but to a much lesser degree than humans. In this sense, humans are distinct from animals as a matter of degree, not of essence. Thus, it is understandable that we are more hesitant to kill and eat those animals which possess more highly developed reflective faculties (with which we thus consider ourselves to have a closer connection) than we are when it comes to other animal species and plants.

Q: Instead of following our instincts blindly, could we not rely on *tradition* (the customs and habits of our culture)?

A: Indeed, that is something we must do to great lengths, since we cannot always be reinventing – we simply wouldn't have the time. Just think of our everyday language. It may permit misunderstandings, present logical traps and other faults, but as a means of communication it serves us quite satisfactorily in most situations.

A great many of the traditions, customs and habits that we follow (usually without much thought, as we have grown into them in the forms in which they were passed on to us) deserve our trust. This has to do with the fact that our ancestors were more or less reasonable beings and that the "groundwork" they have laid is not likely to be a pile of trash – at least, this is what we tacitly assume, and probably with some reason. But with no more than *some*: "Let us hold on to the old, where it is good, and with every hour build the new upon it," said Goethe. "*Where* it is good" – in this "where" lies the problem. We have to put the old to the test and ask, is it ever really good? That something is old, that it belongs to the canon of traditions, customs and habits of our culture, does not mean that it is good. For how long did people think that the world was a disk, the heavens a bell jar above it, with God looking in? That proved untenable, and the forms of life, social order and power structures which had formerly based themselves upon this world view lost their foundation.

Q: If we cannot rely on our instincts and cannot blindly follow tradition, then what is left?

A: Our *critical reasoning*. The Greek work *kritein* means "to differentiate". Above all, our critical reasoning can differentiate between what is correct and what is not; in other words, between *true* and *false*. One might also add those things about which we cannot determine either their truth or their falsity. But this is also a question of truth: Is it true that (for the present, or in principle) we do not know whether or not something is true? "Let your word be yes, yes; no, no", as we find in the Bible.

Of course, we cannot reinvent our critical reasoning every day. That we possess it is something we owe to the "groundwork" laid by our ancestors. That is to say, the tools with which our reasoning performs its critical work have been developed by cultural labor.

Q: But why do we have to know whether a thing is false or not?

A: Certainly not for "academic" reasons, but rather because we could not survive otherwise.

If I do not know whether or not the mushroom I am about to eat is poisonous, I take the risk of dying for my ignorance. If I have erred in calculating the re-entry angle of a space capsule as it returns to earth, it may be that the whole crew will pay for my error with their lives.

Of course, most situations in which the question of truth presents itself are not as dramatic as this. Most are in fact trivial and insignificant: Will it rain or not; should I take an umbrella? How much fuel does the car that I would like to buy consume? Can I afford it? And so on.

Q: Does the question of truth arise only in connection with our knowledge of the world or does it also apply in connection with our actions within it?

A: In both cases. For, on the one hand, we must know: Is it *true* that a space capsule re-entering the atmosphere at an angle of so many degrees and a speed of so many kilometers per hour heats up by so many degrees? On the other hand we must also know: Is it *true* that it would be better if the heat shield around the capsule were twice as thick as it currently is – therefore, that it *should* be made thicker?

Thus, questions of truth appear in the realm in which we need to know *what is the case*, as well as in the realm in which we need to know what we*should and should not do*.

We can call the first realm the realm of "theoretical reason" and the second, the realm of "practical reason".

Q: Can't we simply put aside the question of truth?

A: One can try, certainly. Already in Ancient Greece, some philosophers had asserted that there is no truth, that everything is deception and lies, that truth is at best only "relative". In our own time, too, there are people who defend this position; it is in fact fashionable – which is quite astonishing, for the counter-argument is obvious: If the proposition "there is no truth" means anything at all (and is not simply meaningless grumbling), then it means: "The proposition 'there is no truth' is true". It is clear that, as soon as we take the utterance seriously, it turns out to be self-contradictory. If we don't take it seriously, then there is no point in wasting our time with it. If we meet one of these philosophers of non-truth, we can convince ourselves fairly quickly that it is nothing more than an intellectual game by accompanying them to, for example, their bank and seeing their reaction when the teller states that, after having read this philosopher's latest work about the nonexistence of truth, it is impossible for the bank to know anything for certain about funds received for them, nor can it make any definite assertions about their funds, their account, or anything else of consequence.

Q: But what is wrong with self-contradiction? Don't we sometimes say of a deceased person, in sympathy and even with a bit of admiration, "Even in his contradictions he was great"?

A: We say this because we sometimes find human failings endearing (so long as they are not too serious). We also know of our own individual weaknesses and tend to turn a blind eye to them. It makes our life a little easier. But if we in all seriousness were to accept self-contradiction unconditionally, we would be forced to accept its opposite as well: the *refusal* of self-contradiction; and second, in a serious circumstance, we would not need much time to decide on which side of the argument we stand. Suppose we are, for example, running a construction company and would like to know from the engineer who has constructed our newest bridge whether it can carry the loads that are expected. Suppose he answers "Yes and no". We would surely respond, taken aback or angry, that this is a contradiction, and if he were to insist further on his answer, perhaps propounding the benefits of self-contradiction, we would give him his walking papers.

Q: If we admit that we should not let our actions be steered by our natural instincts, we still have to acknowledge that without our natural *senses* we would not be able to recognize anything or, in any case, that we would not get very far in our search for knowledge.
A. That is correct, particularly the last part of the sentence. If someone had no senses *at all* – how would he perceive anything, and how could we find out from him whether he had perceived anything? On the other hand, it is not the case that the "impressions" that reach us via our senses already have the quality of knowledge – certainly not in a manner that is reliable. Reliable knowledge is obtained only when two further aspects are taken into consideration: The *reason* of the individual (receiving sensual impressions), and the discursive *co-subjectivity* unavoidably inherent in every act of reason. In other words, reliable knowledge always, in this (linguistic) sense, presupposes co-subjectivity.

Q: Could we perhaps unravel this a little? To begin with, why are sensual impressions not immediately reliable knowledge?

A: First of all, because as mere sensory data, sensual impressions are not yet registered or assimilated – they are simply there. The registering and assimilating is the result of an act of reason. The fact that our senses transmit to us the impression of "something" is only possible because the idea of "something" exists in our reason. The notion that our sense data has to do with things that are "there" is something that our reason provides; it is not in the data itself. Kant called this the "concept of substance". Our ability to perceive objects in *space*, that is, as three-dimensional, depends on our having a concept of space. We perceive sequences of events as such only because we can organize our otherwise disconnected impressions according to an idea of *time* – again, this idea is not present in the sense data itself. Kant referred to this as the "forms of perception" – space and time. Further, when we ascertain causal connections between events that we perceive in space and time, these connections are not imminently present in the sense data itself; for this we require the concept of "causality".

When we look at a geometrical drawing of, say, a pyramid or a cube, it might take a while to "figure out" what it is that the lines represent; for example, a pyramid with the apex at the top or pointing downwards. "Ah, now I see it!" we would say. But we've been "seeing" it all along, or at least receiving sense impressions from it; it's just that our visual impressions were not yet processed by our reasoning.

Q: And what does this have to do with co-subjectivity, as mentioned above?

A: It is relevant in at least two respects. Firstly, those concepts and categories we use to integrate sense impressions into our understanding are available to us because we have worked them out not on our own, as isolated individuals, but discursively – that is, with the help of our human co-subjects. The development of concepts which enable us to apprehend reality and thereby obtain knowledge is an important cultural accomplishment.

Another such accomplishment is the use of the so-called logical particles (such as: and, or, if – then, all, none). These, too, are not simply innate to us but must be worked out and learnt discursively. Language, however, always implies the existence of a fellow human being, in the sense of a co-subject of recognition.

By virtue of their participation in the construction of those concepts that make knowledge possible for us, our fellow human beings are inescapably involved in every process of recognition ("Erkenntnis"), even in those that seem to be solitary.

Secondly, our efforts at recognition are dependent, in a rather 'external' sense, on our fellow creatures in that we depend on their suggestions and criticisms. We make errors, and besides, the intellectual capacity of any one person is limited. In both cases, we depend on help from others. The criticisms another might make of things I consider to be true can show me where I have gone wrong. His suggestions might draw my attention to any oversights.

Q: Does this mean there is no "solitary" recognition?

A: There may be, but only in rudimentary form. Even animals which hardly communicate with one another, are able to recognize things. And Kaspar Hauser (a 19th Century German youth, infamous, as he himself asserted in his later life, for spending his youth locked in a darkened dungeon isolated from the outside world, having never been introduced to language) recognized that which was shoved into his cell as food, even though, as the story goes, no one had ever spoken to him. It may be that those communicative faculties of the brain, which are necessary for the working out and refinement of knowledge-enabling concepts, achieve a rudimentary, solitary perception. These abilities must be present in each individual; otherwise they could not be activated in situations of learning and teaching.

Q: Could it not well be that, in diametric opposition to this, all recognition only takes place in the consciousness of the individual, that there is no world around him, but rather that it is all just an illusion?

A: This, like the question "Can't we simply put aside the question of truth?", is merely a "paper doubt" (a doubt which is not meant genuinely), as the American philosopher Peirce would have said. This sort of objection is familiar to us by now, and the reply is still the same: First, the objection falls into its own trap, for if everything is imagined, then so is this objection – which of course was not the object of the objection. Second, suppose we should in fact call the world and everything in it "imagined", this would change nothing, except the amount of verbiage used to describe the world. Third, we could again go to the bank with any advocate of this idea and wait for his reaction when the teller advises him that he is only imagining the deposit of his salary into his account yesterday.

Q: So in attempting to discover the facts of the world around us, we are (if this attempt is more than rudimentary) dependent on our fellow human beings?

A: Yes. Even in posing the most simple question, like "Is this mushroom poisonous?", we transcend our subjectivity in various ways: We turn to someone else (from whom we hope to obtain the knowledge that we ourselves lack), and in doing so, we use the medium of language, which we have acquired through a long process of communication with other human beings.

Q: Could we not simply stop asking questions?

A: No. We *need* the information that we want to get but cannot acquire on our own. But even supposing someone, as an experiment, would completely refrain from posing questions, in order to demonstrate the possibility of this task to his discussion partner, who in contrast defends its impossibility (that inter-subjectivity is unavoidable) – even this demonstration would be a demonstration *for* someone, that is, it would entail an inter-subjective context.

Furthermore, we could not maintain this position (that it is possible to live without the asking of questions) if we had during our lives, e.g. as children, really held and practiced this view! As children, we pestered our parents and others around us to the point of exasperation with questions like “Why is that?”, “What’s that called?”, “What does he mean?”, and so on.

Without having passed through this early learning process, with its endless questions and answers, we would not now, as adults, be able to take part in a discussion about the avoidability or unavoidability of inter-subjectivity. Had we not posed seriously meant questions earlier, we would still be the small, ignorant creatures we once were.

Q: Does every question really have to be “serious”?

A: Of course not. We can also ask questions playfully, only pretending to search for an answer, and so on. Yet even these playful questions are comprehensible as such – that is, as “playful” and not “serious” – only when we first understand what we mean by “serious”. One has to be able to say seriously, “Believe me, I didn’t mean to ask this question seriously”. Or, said the other way round, we need to be seriously aware of what we mean when we use the word “playful”.

And here we can repeat the argumentation of the previous answer: One could certainly decide, as a thought experiment, never to ask serious questions (strictly speaking this won’t work, since a world in which we ask no serious questions could not even be perceived in a manner that is anything more than rudimentary – because any more than the most rudimentary perception requires us to pose seriously meant questions). As we can see from the trivial example of the possibly poisonous mushrooms, our life expectancy would be short if we really were to take seriously the policy of not being “serious” – and here, at least, we would unavoidably confront the seriousness of the word “serious”.

Q: What leads us (as early as in childhood) to ask questions?

A: Whatever the cause, in doing so we exercise an ability that is part of our makeup as rational beings. Why the world, our life and our reason (and therefore this capability of asking questions) should exist – this is something we don’t know. In asking “Why?”, however, we are (reflectively) referred to the categories of world, life, reason (and with it freedom) as irreducible concepts, which we implicitly recognize in the very act of questioning. Such questions about implicit conditions – in other words, the reflection about "conditions for the possibility of..." – are, as mentioned before, what Kant called "transcendental". In this light we can say: *Transcendental reflection is the pragmaticanswer (always implicit in any speech act) to the three fundamental questions about existence that have no substantiveanswers.*

Q: A propos freedom: Does it really exist? What about the opposing view that everything is predetermined – even processes in the brain, which is supposedly the source of our "freedom"? There are many who defend this view.

A: This is again a "paper doubt". And again the same answer:

1. If everything is predetermined, then so is this view. But this cannot be the intention. In order to use this idea in a discussion, it must first be considered an argument, which in itself presupposes a kind of freedom of thought.
2. But if we simply overrule this objection (1) and declare everything (even argumentation) to be predetermined, we come to no meaningful result, for then everything in our world is just as it has always been, except that we have the additional linguistic burden of calling everything predetermined.
3. Let us once again follow an adherent of this view to his bank and observe his reaction when the teller informs him that an inescapable chain of cause and effect has determined that yesterday's salary deposit cannot be paid out.

Q: Let's return to the question of unavoidable inter-subjectivity. How can we more concretely describe this inter-subjectivity, which is contained in every simple question? What sort of relationship do I enter into when I ask someone a question?

A: By asking a question, I implicitly recognize a) the existence of certain anthropological givens and, at the same time, b) the validity of certain rules of speech acts in the sense of mutually accepted rights and duties.

Q: For example?

A: Such anthropological givens (a) which I necessarily accept in asking a question are, for example, that:

1. I *need* a partner in discourse because I don't know the answer myself, or at least don't know it for sure;
2 My partner in discourse is a being whom I assume to be capable of answering me (hence, that he or she is to this extent rational);
3 He or she can understand me, that is, realizes that he or she is being addressed with a question.

With every question I ask, I necessarily accept (b) basic shared discourse-related responsibilities, for example with respect to:

1. *Choice of words*: There are certain*rules* governing the use of words which I agree to follow and which I expect to be followed by my partner in discourse;
2 *Sincerity:* The question I pose is meant sincerely and I expect that my partner will answer me with similar sincerity. This also means that he will tell me when he actually knows no answer, has only a partial one, or has doubts about it;
3 *Trans-subjective openness:* When my partner can only give an unsatisfactory answer or no answer at all to my question, I can expect that he will help me find *someone* who can answer it, since he understands that he, as an individual, must put himself second in the pursuit of truth; in other words, that every question posed seriously is in fact addressed not specifically to him, but to *every* rational being and thus is meant to be virtually universalistic.
4 *Justification:* I can expect that my partner answers not only with a statement, but that he is prepared to tell me *why* he thinks this statement is the correct (true) answer.
5 *Argumentative discourse:* I can expect my discursive partner not only to give me the justifications for his answer, but also to be willing to respond to objections that I may present; in other words, to be willing to enter into an argumentative dialogue with me, one in which justifications and counter-justifications are weighed against one another.
6 *Rules of argumentation:* Such a dialogue is only possible in the framework of certain rules of logic, and the participants must agree to adhere to these.

7 *Openness to revision:* When new information is received which has the potential to affect the outcome of the argument, the participants must be willing to take this into account and, if applicable, to revise any conclusions they had previously come to.
8 *Aiming toward consensus:* When there are no further arguments to be presented and the dialogue thus appears to be at an end, both participants agree to regard the result of the dialogue up to this point as the (possibly preliminary) answer to their posed question – this result is the *truth* of the matter as they have so far been able to determine.

Q: Are there any more anthropological givens or responsibilities of communication that we might add to these lists?
A: It's possible that others can be identified. In any case, the above lists are not intended to be definitive.

Q: Would it not be very important to methodologically reconstruct such rules of dialogue, starting from the simplest speech acts and proceeding to elaborate linguistic structures, in order to make clear to us the mutual rights and duties that they entail?
A: Yes. Indeed, Wilhelm Kamlah and Paul Lorenzen, the founders of the so-called Erlangen School, attempted this in their "Logical Propaedeutics" (1967), both for "theoretical" propositions (those that describe facts) and for "practical" propositions (those that say what should be done). However, Kamlah and Lorenzen were not aware of the transcendental-pragmatic presuppositions described above. Their approach was: *If* people want to talk to one another reasonably, then they can do this by following a certain set of rules, namely that which was described in "Logical Propaedeutics". They had not yet recognized that the posing of seriously meant questions (implicit in the *conditio humana*) necessarily entails a mutual acceptance of a set of rules (which are reconstructed in "Logical Propaedeutics").

Q: Could we describe this "set of rules" as a kind of "minimal ethics"?
A: We might well do so. However, this form of ethics is not really so "minimal"! We shall later examine the practical and political consequences which would surely follow if we genuinely were to fulfill the conditions posed for an undistorted dialogue in search of truth.

Q: Can we summarize the important points?

A: Yes.

1. As human beings, we are existentially dependent on our willingness and ability to ask serious questions.
2 In asking a simple, seriously meant question, we implicitly accept the universal validity of fundamental ethical rules.
3 In this respect we humans are all equal. "Equal" here means that we, as potential dialogue partners, have the same rights and duties.

Q: Is it possible to derive from these merely formal rules any substantive conclusions concerning our actions in concrete situations?

A: No, we cannot *derive* anything substantive *from* them, but we can *work with* these rules by applying them to concrete situations. That is what they are there for.

Take as an example the question as to whether the sale of cigarettes to minors should be forbidden. This question cannot be answered by someone whose sole function is to ensure that the formal rules of argumentative dialogue are being respected. If he were to play a part in this discussion, he would also need to have the relevant knowledge and expertise.

As a side note: To characterize the rules as "merely" formal is misleading. The rules are not "merely" formal (in the negative sense); rather, they have the *virtue* of being "merely", that is, purely, formal.

Q: And why should that be an advantage?

A: If we were to consider contents (values) as the basis of ethics, and if those values were to conflict with one another (for example, in the case of different views about whether one or the other substantive proposition or value can or should or must be seen as most relevant), then these conflicts would not be resolvable, except by referring to supposedly "higher" values or propositions – which again could stand in conflict with one another – or by violent means. Violence is in fact the "procedure" through which such substantive conflicts are often resolved. In the case of a conflict between states which each defend conflicting values, this "procedure" is war. Yet, in an age in which weapons of mass destruction and global environmental threats are spreading, war is not an option we can afford. War is now coupled with a previously unknown risk – an unrestrained modern war, fought with all military means available, would eradicate the human race, or leave little of it behind.

The search for non-military means of resolving conflicts is thus an existential necessity. The Charter of the United Nations recognizes this necessity in its general prohibition of war. It allows wars only when legitimated by the Security Council or in cases of immediate self-defense (and in this case, authorization by the Security Council must be obtained as soon as possible).

In the Security Council meetings no shooting takes place, only talking, and the talking adheres to a predefined, commonly agreed upon formal procedure.

Q: Do not the supposedly primary, formal, basic rules actually presuppose value statements, for example the postulates of "seriousness" (of questions) and "equality" (of all human beings)?

A: It is true that the statements "You *should* ask serious questions (if you want the truth)!" and "You *should* accept the arguments of all persons with equal readiness (if you want the truth)!" are ethical postulates (general normative statements). They are not, however, *ascriptions* of value. They are not arbitrarily or randomly chosen. Rather, their acceptance is an inescapable precondition of the effort to find truth through dialogue; they cannot be denied. Even in attempting to do so, one would have to implicitly make use of them in order to explain and defend this denial.

Thus, the objection that was intended in the question above turns out to be, in reality, a valid demonstration of the minimal ethics inherent in it (as in any seriously meant question). This minimal ethics is not imposed and cannot be derived; it shows itself when, through transcendental reflection, we consider the conditions of possibility inherent in every serious question.

Q: Coming back to the alternative which was just mentioned, "solving conflicts by dialogue or by violence (war)": will mankind succeed in solving its conflicts in a way that does not bring about its complete or near destruction?

A: When we consider the degree of stupidity, religion, ideology and other forms of *un*reason rampant in human society, as well as our aggressiveness and short-sightedness, the prognosis can't be good.

Q: Then there is nothing to hope for?

A: There are indeed grounds for hope, and it is in these that we must put all of our efforts, on all fronts, and not let ourselves be deterred by setbacks.

A large part of humanity and even heads of state have understood that they will only cause future catastrophes and possibly even their own demise if they take no decisive action against existing risks. This insight is due less to high-minded moral principles than to the sober reckoning of long-term self-interest. But even that is better than no insight at all!

In the United Nations and its subordinate organizations, states have created a most important global institution, in which they can resolve their conflicts within the framework of formal procedures; at least, they can attempt to do so. In more than a few cases, indeed in very important and life-endangering cases, conflicts have in fact been settled in this manner. It is important to pursue this path further!

Another reason for hope is the fact that multilateral agreements between states have been put in place (outside the UN), meant to mitigate or eliminate global environmental and military threats.

Finally, a third ground for hope can be seen in the measures taken independently by a state to contribute to the attainment of these same global goals.

Q: We have seen that, strictly taken, truth can only be found in an ideal communicative situation of the sort indicated above. But where in the world can such a situation exist? Is that not merely a well-intentioned utopia?

A: In the first place, it cannot be a utopia because truth *cannot* be found in any other way.

"U-topia" means "no place". As is evidenced by the immense and ever growing collection of knowledge we have available today, there must be *some* "place" where it is possible to obtain knowledge (truth).

This place is "anticipation". In our truth-seeking dialogues, we act as if we were already in the "ideal communicative situation"; we anticipate, in particular, possible counter-arguments that, theoretically, could come from any rational being.

This anticipation usually works in everyday life. Yet, one never knows whether or not a counter-argument or further relevant information might still exist in the mind of someone who was not able to express it (either because he had been hindered, by means of power or simply by a lack of communicative infrastructure). Considering this last point, it is evident that even if, in a thought-experiment, we were to imagine that all restraints were eliminated and an ideal "Christian-communist" society – free from domination, based on the postulates of equality, freedom and solidarity – were fully realized, we would still find it impossible in practice to verify whether all possible counter-arguments have really been taken into consideration. In other words, even in the best of all possible worlds, anticipation would still be necessary.

And it is all the more necessary in a human world-society permeated to such a great degree and depth by power structures as ours!

Q: Returning to Kant and his subjective, pre-dialogical concept of *reason*: What are the consequences of this concept having been conceived without reference to the necessity of such a utopian counterfactual anticipation of an ideal communicative situation?

A: For Kant, reason is a mental capability of the *individual*. And the Enlightenment is a call, a hope, an appeal to individuals. *Sapere aude*! – Dare to know! If the world is to become more reasonable, this appeal must be heard and followed by individuals throughout the world.

All the same, Kant entertains no illusions about the prospects of this appeal. Further progressions, even significant ones, are conceivable for him. Working toward this end is what gives sense and purpose to life. But that the *world* will in fact fully become reasonable – this is a naivety that he cannot permit himself. "From such crooked wood as that which man is made of, nothing straight can be fashioned," he wrote. What remains is a "regulative idea", a postulate that can never be fully realized. The fact that we have the courage, in our own finite lives, to invest our efforts into attaining a meaning which is ultimately beyond our grasp; to entrust one's own, limited span to an infinity that lies beyond one's own horizon – in this he sees something religious. More precisely, for him it is this which will remain of religion if it seeks a place "within the limits of reason alone" (as explained in his book of this title). The Kantian concept of religion is in any case not bound to any transcendent world; it does not create any bridges to a world beyond. It rather establishes, on the basis of the logic of reason, a connection to the unattainable, utopian *aim* of reasoned activity in this world.

Transcendental-pragmatic philosophy can get along without this concept of religion.

Kant was generous enough to continue to use the word "religion", even though this was in a sense which deprived it of its original claim to transcendence. Like Kant, transcendental-pragmatic philosophy admits that the realization of reason in the world *is* a utopian project, in the sense that it is based on counter-factual anticipation, but beyond Kant it observes that it is nevertheless at the same time *factually given*, insofar as this anticipation takes place and *must* take place.

Q: Is the principle of virtual equality and reciprocity between all human beings, implicitly recognized in every seriously posed question, not something that stands in *stark contrast* to the existing *political and economic relations of power*? Is it not thus an ever-present call to overcome these same relations?

A: Evidently this is the case. For, even if we could assume ideal, well-meaning patriarchs as our rulers, this situation would still be inadequate, since, first, we can never know with certainty what the subjects under such a ruler would in fact have said or wanted, except by asking them, and, second, even the well-meaning anticipations of a patriarch are nothing more than a mild form of paternalism, a tacit hindering of rational beings in their efforts at self-realization.

Q: What does the fact that the truth-seeking individual is inescapably dependent on virtually universalistic dialogue with *equals* mean for the (power-determined) political institutions of the state?

A: It encourages a call for ever greater democratization (in the sense of overcoming domination) and thus recognizes the need to break down power relations continually (in whichever empirical form they might appear or reappear).

This is a never-ending task. At best, we can conceive of it as gradually moving closer toward the goal, always accompanied by the prospect of reversals and setbacks.

Freedom is a regulative idea; there is no "master plan" to achieve it. Above all, it cannot be achieved by a plan which aims to do so in a short time, nor by one that claims to know the *singular* cause of domination (such as the possession of the means of production) and hopes to eliminate it quickly and forcefully, once and for all.

Q: And what does this mean for the *economic* realm?

A: What has been said of political relations can be reiterated with respect to economic relations, for in our time (probably to a greater extent than in earlier times) the genuine political power lies in the hands of the economic heavyweights. This is true in two respects:

(a) The effects of *economic* decisions drastically reverberate throughout other areas of life, and (b), on top of this, *political* decisions are, from the beginning, influenced by or tailored toward the interests of these economic heavyweights.

It is from these internal structures of economic life and their influence on society, both nationally and globally, that an essential inequality arises among people; at least, this is one of its main sources. This is not to say that the economic system seeks to inhibit the search for truth. It is in fact heavily reliant on information; it needs *knowledge*, knowledge that is well-founded and reliable, up to date and open to criticism.

The economic system by nature, however, is only concerned with knowledge useful for the pursuit of its interests. Yet – and this is the decisive point – its interests are not per se those of society, nor, much less, of humanity. "What is good for General Motors is good for America" – this is not correct. And even if it were, it is not for General Motors to decide! Whether the US, or, more correctly, its people, will be benefited by the advancement of General Motors' interests – that is something for the people to decide.

The German Constitution or Basic Law declares in article 14, paragraph 2 that "Ownership entails obligation. It shall also serve the common good." ("Eigentum verpflichtet. Sein Gebrauch soll zugleich dem Wohle der Allgemeinheit dienen.") As such, ownership is subordinate to the common good – it is obliged to serve it. What the common good is, however, is not for the economic system to decide, because it is itself only a part of the whole. The common good is something that can be determined only by the entire sovereign — in this case, by the German people as a whole.

Turning Article 14, Paragraph 2 of the Constitution into democratic, lived reality is the political-economic variant of the regulative idea of *freedom* formulated as a constitutional mandate.

Q: Is it not naïve to hope that individual states can enforce the conditions for genuinely free economic structures when confronted by the enormous power of globally functioning economic entities?

A: Marx was of this opinion (that it would be naïve) and for this reason he saw the need for a *world* revolution. Lenin's experiment of creating "socialism in a single country" appears, in retrospect, to have proved him right. Its result was not a greater level of freedom, but of terror.

Q: Should we then give up this hope?

A: In reality, "hope" is not the appropriate word. It is not a matter of having a utopian dream, but rather of soberly recognizing that in order for the human being to survive, it *cannot* live without truth, and that the pursuit of truth presupposes freedom and equality, and that therefore all kinds of repression and inequality hinder the human being in attaining its full humanity. Hence, gradually overcoming these hindrances is a necessary postulate, a "regulative idea" – not a naïve hope.

Q: This may be right in theory. Yet the problem remains: What can individual states do to counter today's globally acting economic forces?

A: Again, we must bear in mind that this task is an on-going one; neither a quick nor a final solution is to be expected. However, as blind expansion and exploitation, on one side, increasingly place humanity's chances of survival at risk (including, of course, those of the economic system), so too will social and governmental forces, on the other side, increasingly mobilize to demand the subordination of economic profit interests to general survival interests. This is once again due less to high moral standards than to the sober reckoning of long-term self-interest. Important steps (though up till now inadequate ones) have been taken in this direction. The largest meeting of world leaders in our history, the environmental conference in Rio de Janeiro, and the ecological principles enunciated at the conference in Kyoto, are two examples.

Q: Does the democratization of economic life mean the socialization or nationalization of the means of production?

A: In the sense of Article 14, Paragraph 2, "demo-cratization" means that economic activities shall also *serve the common good* – whereby the common good reflects the will of the *demos* (the people of the state), and "shall serve" reflects *kratein*, "to rule". Even the various kinds of socialization or nationalization of the means of production, or of parts of them, offer no guarantee that they will then serve the common good. On the other hand, the energy set free by private egotism, when subject to certain rules and restrictions, can certainly serve the common good. Between the poles of pure private ownership and pure state ownership, many intermediate forms can be conceived. Which mixture of these many conceivable forms is most effective and best serves the common good cannot, however, be expressed in a simple formula. Not only is it impossible to present, once and for all, a single, all-encompassing definition of "common good", it is also impossible to define a single strategy for forms of ownership to best serve it. This is the main topic of the never-ending democratic discourse.

Q: Political institutions and forms of ownership in economic life may well be important, but in the end aren't they merely outward manifestations – isn't the eternal struggle for freedom ultimately dependent on the attitudes and inner values of people?

A: Certainly these formal institutions are only empty shells if they are not filled with life by the convictions of human beings (more precisely, by sufficiently strong convictions of a sufficiently large number of people).

On the other hand, it is the goal of enlightenment and education – which are directed at developing these inner values – to in the end bring about changes in societal reality (in the outer circumstances of life). Enlightenment and education cannot be understood in the terms of "art for art's sake".

The relationship between these two aspects must be seen dialectically; there is an interaction between them:

The more democratically the formal outer institutions are structured, the greater are the prospects for a fruitful further development of education and enlightenment, and as these become more differentiated and more highly developed, these outer institutions will be subject to increasing pressure to adapt to the higher level of culture attained by society.

Of course, there is no guarantee that this upward dialectical spiral will actually take place.

Q: Must we not rather fear that those who have an interest in the maintenance and further expansion of existing power structures – such as (and above all) the captains of industry and those who represent them in politics and in the media – will use their positions to counter possible threats to their power, and even to ideologically influence people in such a way that they willingly help to *augment* the power of their rulers?

A: Of course. It would in fact be strange if things were otherwise. This is how it has always been, and always will be. All the same, some portions of humanity have succeeded in making significant progress in the struggle against arbitrary power over the course of history! The democratic *Rechtsstaat* (a state under the rule of law) and the institutions of social solidarity are salient examples of this progress – despite the many serious shortcomings that may be inherent in them.

Q: What are the means through which power is exercised?

A: Those which have always been used, for example:

- Keeping people ignorant, particularly by denying them a proper education, at least in
- those areas from which threats to the dominant powers could arise (that is, by arranging that the dominated remain unaware or at least as little aware as possible, of their true circumstances of life).
- Distracting the public from the real problems, for example, through sensationalist journalism on irrelevant topics.
- Deceiving the public with lies and half-truths.
- Using religion to make the public believe that the conditions under which they live are ordained by God.
- Making them believe that the conditions under which they live are unalterably constrained by necessity.
- Ridiculing and suppressing all theories, persons or forces which show the public the true workings behind power structures, and which reveal the possibility of altering these structures, thus threatening their hold on power.

Modern power-holders have more efficient, far-reaching (virtually totalitarian) and refined means at their disposal for influencing the masses than were available in earlier times – in particular, the mass media. Through these means it has become possible to reduce open violence and symbolic displays of power. The power-holders are no longer (so strongly) required to assert themselves with brute force; their power is lodged in the struc-

tures and, more importantly, they have more efficient methods to govern the minds of the people. "Soft power" is more effective and 'harder' than "hard power". In contrast to earlier times – when ostentatious, even exhibitionistic displays of the splendor of the powerful (the aristocracy and clergy) were not only a means of self-representation but also of intimidation of the dominated – modern power no longer shows itself; it vanishes behind the mirrored façades of the banks and administrative buildings.
Those in power are so self-assured that they will even permit criticism if it does not constitute a real danger to their position. In this way they create the impression of openness, tolerance and alleged freedom. Herbert Marcuse called this "repressive tolerance".

Q: Along with the freedoms of speech, of assembly and of the press, academic freedom, that is, of teaching and research, is one of the great achievements of the modern constitutional democratic state. Could it not be expected that academics, especially in the fields of humanities and philosophy, would declare precisely this basic discrepancy between existing power structures and the individual's intrinsic claim to freedom and equality (something essential to the dignity of every rational being) to be one of their main concerns?

A: In any case this discrepancy exists latently, whether academics take notice of it or not. What we might call a muffled appeal inevitably goes out to the forces of domination, one inextricably linked to any search for truth – a quiet and for the most part *unconscious* challenge. For these forces, whatever they might be called, what matters most is to prevent the latent challenge against them from rising into *conscious* awareness, or, when it is too late for that and it starts to become articulated, to suppress and disarm it. The rapid watering-down of the idea and institutions of academic freedom, as well as their increasing subjection to economic interests and private profit, has already begun to attack core premises of relatively free basic research. Contemporary politics (whose task, by its own account, is to serve the common good) has largely failed to defend the academic system – most noticeably in areas such as engineering, natural sciences and parts of the social sciences – from being exploited for economic ends, to the extent that it routinely claims that the subjugation of science to the interests of economic powers serves the common good.

But even those areas of academia that are *less* directly susceptible to exploitation– certain other sections of the social sciences, the humanities and the great philosophical schools of our time – do not present a threat to power. Not only because they are materially dependent, which makes discontent or open rebellion appear inopportune (that is, on external grounds), but also because of their internal ideological structures.

"Critical Rationalism" denies the existence of positive truth (there is only trial and error); "Postmodernism" negates the "modern" concept of reason and claims the existence of a plurality of forms thereof; "Scientism" restricts itself to a logical critique of the natural sciences; "Analytical Philosophy of Language", for its part, is concerned with subtle analysis of speech acts.

This is not the place to expand on and justify these judgments. A somewhat more detailed presentation of them follows in Part II.

The real scandal, namely the basic discrepancy described above, is not something they address – apart from a few individuals like the linguist Noam Chomsky. It's a good time to be in power, one might say. But every independently thinking individual cannot help but feel embarrassed by this situation. Who today dares to speak up and put the powerful in their place? Well, the German Constitution has done it, and in the past, the late Pope John Paul II did it, too.

Q: So then, what should democratic institutions and economic structures look like? Who should decide what, when and how?

A: These questions are of course of quite decisive importance.

At the same time we must recognize that they cannot be posed *once* and answered *once*. Debating the best possible answers to them is a never-ending task which must be attempted within the forum of the whole of society.

Ethics, if it is not to exceed the bounds of its competence, cannot take a position on substantive questions. Its task is to remind the participants of a dialogue (that is, society) that if they are seriously interested in reliable answers, they will then (to the extent that is possible within a given culture) have to organize their dialogue (the societal debate) in a manner which allows the attainment of these answers.

It is evident (and has already been mentioned) that the existing societies and states, and beyond these, the world community, are far from fulfilling these elementary demands.

Q: Hasn't ethics made life a little too easy for itself?

A: The *foundation* of ethics (in the sense of reflection on the reciprocal rights and duties necessarily inherent and universally recognized in every seriously posed question) is, as we have seen, easy to comprehend. One might say it is obvious (or, more precisely, "self-evident" – a term which more clearly expresses its self-referential, self-reflecting aspect).

It would indeed be surprising and even puzzling if the foundation of ethics was not, at least in principle, easily understandable to all – if, so to speak, we would need a Ph. D. in practical philosophy before we are able to "get it". A philosopher colleague, on seeing a book recommended to him after one of his lectures, said that it was "much too thick to be true". That there are nevertheless people who write such thick books on ethics, and even do so professionally, has to do "merely" with the fact that, in traditional debates of practical philosophy, important and serious currents of thought exist which do not recognize this "self-evidence" – quite apart from the necessity of defending the standpoint of reflective reason (the ethically relevant self-understanding of reason) against *religious* and *ideological* thought.

Institutions, as the British sociologist C. N. Parkinson noted, often if not nearly always have a tendency to become inflated and ineffective, and to acquire a mentality of "art for art's sake". A good portion of academic debates regarding ethics may be of this nature.

Confronting the diverging positions of practical philosophy and of the various forms of religious and ideological thought is certainly not "easy". One has to understand and analyze these positions *critically* in order to evaluate what is sustainable and what is not. A certain amount of empathy as well as expertise (scholarship) and critical analytical competence are required, along with a proper systematic position.

It is also not an "easy" task to disseminate these insights through the avenues of education and enlightenment. In education it is especially important to accept fully a child's intrinsic inquisitive nature, and not to stifle continual questioning by referring to the child's supposed immaturity, to authorities, doctrines of belief, ideological axioms or fixed ideas. On the contrary, questioning needs to be accepted and encouraged to the point that the conditions which make questioning itself possible (self-reflectively) become the object of the questions.

A third task that is by no means "easy" is the ongoing effort to adequately respond to the tension between, on the one hand, the necessary postulates of freedom and equality which are inherent in speech acts and underlie societal structures, and on the other hand, the historically variant forms of domination. Herein lies the most direct confrontation with social powers. To ensure that those elements of society struggling for enlightenment are not fighting a losing battle, it is essential that the already achieved democratic institutions, e.g. freedom of speech, of assembly, parliamentarianism, and the legal and social institutions respectively of the "constitutional state" and the "welfare state", be defended and extended.

Q: Will there ever be an "end to history", in the sense of a final attainment of freedom and solidarity?

A: The idea of an "end to history" probably belongs to the realm of religious or ideological eschatology. In our world, *salvation* is not in sight. We must continually look for concrete *solutions* - solutions that draw their meaning, however, from being oriented by the regulative idea of freedom (in loftier terms, by the ideal of human dignity), or, more soberly, by our endeavor to approximate gradually the reality of human life to the principles of universality and reciprocity necessarily recognized in every simple serious question.

It would be naïve to suppose that this tension could ever come to an end. All too easily, the preachers of brotherly love turn into terrifying inquisitors; all too easily, the fighters for the abolition of the state become totalitarian bureaucrats; all too easily, the defenders of social solidarity fall into neo-liberalism, and so on. The task of enlightenment has no "end".

Q: But isn't this impulse of enlightenment in itself naïvely idealistic?

A: Giving it up would mean giving up the endeavor of "becoming human". For, only to the extent that we can freely unfold our capacity for reason, can we actually realize our humanity. Furthermore, giving up the postulates of philosophical enlightenment would demean the thousands of years of human cultural labor, the painful but rousing struggle for understanding. The work of enlightenment is not naïve — it is our only hope!

But, strictly speaking, it is not even in our power to give it up; simply asking the question seriously of whether it is not naïve, implies that the questioner — whether or not he knows or wants it — accepts the core principle of its program. A call to give up that program would thus mean nothing more than that the speaker has not understood his own situation as a rational being. Precisely *this* would be naïve (because it lacks self-reflection).

Historical Part

Q: In the first, systematic part, it has become clear that the insights concerning the conditions of the possibility of human knowledge, and the therein implied ethical consequences, are accessible to every rational human being, without requiring any philosophical education – so to speak, from a standing start. Does it then make sense to concern ourselves with the history (which over long stretches may be quite disappointing) of how these insights have been won over the course of some two and a half thousand years?

A: Quite certainly. And for at least three reasons:

Firstly, because only in this way can we become fully aware of how difficult it really was to advance toward these insights (in spite of all misdirection, repression and setbacks) and of how we must therefore treasure these accomplishments!

Secondly, because we can make use of history as a kind of quarry – that is, in those cases where, historically, questions were posed and answers were given that can be useful to us in the present day, but which have been forgotten over the course of time.

And, thirdly, because the writing of history can have an identity-building function: We know ourselves better, when we know our history. That is true for us as individuals, as members of a group, and for us as humanity as a whole.

When we want to know who it is that we are talking to, one thing we will certainly ask about is his or her life history. Job applicants present themselves to potential employers by offering their CV. Thus, a *nation* constitutes itself (mainly) by telling itself a certain narrative that it regards as explaining how it, as a nation, came to be. (This, moreover, suggests that the self-understanding of an individual or group stands in an evolving, dialectic relation to that which the individual or group understands as its history.)

Q: But what is the "identity" of the human being; what is it to be human?

A: Reflecting on the conditions of possibility of knowledge (as they are, for example, inescapably implicit in the act of asking precisely that question "What is it to be human?") yields an answer. "Know thyself" stood written over the Oracle at Delphi, and for Kant, this was above all the central question of philosophy: "What is the human being?" The "Cogito ergo sum" ("I think, therefore I am") of Descartes, too, is self-reflective and transcendental – that is, it reflects on the conditions of possibility of knowledge.

The history of the mistakes and advances made in the endeavor to answer this question (that is, the history of philosophy) must therefore be understood as essential for the historical construction of the identity of humankind as a thinking species.

Q: It seems unlikely that humankind first posed the question about its identity only when it was engraved over the Oracle at Delphi.

A: Of course, in "pre-philosophic" times people also had a need to understand and represent themselves in the light of their specific identity as human beings. This they did in their myths, as well as in other ways. In Greek, *mythos* means story, or narration. In these stories from time immemorial, human tribes have situated their origins and current existence within a cosmological order, or at least within contexts which transcend their immediate environments, so as to lend their own existence some kind of purpose and meaning.

The transition from mythos to philosophy, then, is the transition from tribal-specificity to human-generality; especially insofar as it represents the transition from the unreflective telling and passing on of stories to conscious reflection: What are we doing when we tell these stories? Why do we do it? And then, further: What is to be made of these stories? Are they really true?

Once the question of truth is aimed at the myths, a reflective distancing from them and from the world they present comes into effect. And, simultaneously, the horizon is opened from the unconscious realm of tribal story to a conscious universalism.

Q: Why did the ancient Greeks name this enterprise "philosophy"?

A: Let me preface this by saying that the name certainly has its origins in Ancient Greece and as such belongs to the European culture. But the use of this term should not suggest that philosophy, in the sense of reflective enterprise, is limited to the European culture. As one can easily imagine, "philosophy" in this sense also arose in other advanced civilizations – above all, in China. The Greek term, in any case, hits the core of the matter pretty well: to be a philosopher means to be a *friend* of wisdom (insight, or truth). But one is only a friend to the extent that one endeavors to be so. At the point where I am no longer interested in the person whose friend I claim to be, when I am no longer making an effort – at that point the friendship is extinguished. Most importantly, I do not own my friend. Were I to own him, he would be my slave and with that, an object placed once and for all in my possession by a bill of sale. He would lose his character as a subject, and no further endeavors would be necessary on my part.

Precisely this is what the Greeks must have had in mind: the effort to find wisdom (truth) can never cease; we never "possess" wisdom or truth – then it would be dogma, as one sees in religion.

Q: Isn't the history of philosophy merely a miserable and haphazard collection of doctrines, mistaken ideas, confusions, half-truths, misunderstandings and failed communication that has spread randomly throughout the world over the course of time? Is it not really more of a chaos of confusion than an orderly advancing development, a coherent unfolding of reason?

A: I would venture that it is both. Of course, it would be nicer and more comfortable for us if it were neatly ordered, and if we could, without too much interpretive struggling, see it as a kind of staircase, at the top of which we now stand (or at least could stand, if we wanted to). It appears to be the case, however, that here, as in nature, an immense variety of specimens are produced of which only a few can survive. (Yet this is an external view of the matter. It ignores the internal viewpoint which suggests that every philosophical position and its justification must be measured against the standard of truth already set *in the very process* of its development; they do not simply arise randomly to then succumb to some equally random fatal circumstance of life, like species in nature.)

A different comparison is perhaps more fruitful: the philosopher Ludwig Wittgenstein once evoked the image of philosophical clouds which eventually condense to a drop of truth.

Q: Why did this transition from mythos to philosophy come about?

A: Why it came about is probably not something we can reconstruct historically or theoretically. What we can say with certainty, however, is that it was not one definitive event. There was a beginning, but there is no end. To continue this transition is a never-ending task of thinking humanity, whose history is essentially the history of its effort to further this process. The kinds of threatening reversals that can intervene are illustrated all too well by the political myths of the last century (particularly the myths of National Socialism), but also by the nationalistic-religious myths of our own time (for example, religious fundamentalism in the United States, whose proponents see themselves as being in "God's own country", or, with a biological background, the Zionist myth of the chosen status of the Jewish nation with respect to God, and finally, without a specifically nationalistic component, but no less frightening, Islamic fundamentalism.)

Q: Can we determine, without resorting to interpretive struggle, elements of progress in the history of philosophy?

A: If that were not possible, we would certainly have cause for despair. The Procrustean bed is hopefully not necessary to this end, though, in the history of exegesis, hermeneutics and interpretation, it is one of the most popular and most often used tools: Procrustes lay in wait for passers-by and let only those who would fit into his bed continue on; if they did not, he would saw off the parts that were too long or stretch them so that they fit.

The following section attempts to sketch broadly some of those aspects of the history of philosophy that can be comprehended, without resorting to the Procrustean bed, as successive efforts to find ever better answers to the fundamental question of philosophy. The focus (in varying proportions) will be on aspects of:

- Ancient Greek philosophy (Plato, Aristotle)
- Christianity
- Renaissance and Protestantism
- Empirical Enlightenment
- Kantian Enlightenment
- Philosophy of History (Hegel, Marx); and more briefly:
- 'Ich'-philosophy of German Idealism
- Analytical philosophy (Vienna Circle)
- Critical Rationalism (Popper), and
- Post-Modernism.

Q: Couldn't that kind of list lead to confusion?

A: I'll try to avoid that by addressing the same question to each epoch or school of thought and by trying to define the weaknesses and advantages of their respective responses. In this way, it should become clear how they might be related, that is, to what extent later epochs attempted to correct particular deficits of their predecessors.

Q: And what is this unifying question?

A: As said above, it is *the* central philosophical question: What is truth? How can we find a secure orientation? It is the question concerning the possibility of knowledge.

Q: But many important names and schools are missing from your list!

A: True, but that should not be misunderstood as disregard. The purpose of the list is merely to set up a systematic and a historical basis, a kind of framework, which can be filled out later or adapted by every reader. The idea is to cut a few paths through the forest as an aid to the philosophically uninitiated, who often find it hard to see the wood for the trees.

Q: Won't this journey through the history of philosophy produce a rather superficial image?

A: The point of such a survey is not to present an up-to-date overview of current work in philosophy, epoch by epoch, thinker by thinker. But it should nevertheless not be superficial. At least, the question which shapes it is certainly not. If the broad outline of the answers that will emerge is correct, then hopefully its main intention will have been achieved.

Q: Then let's begin with *Plato*. What is his answer to the fundamental philosophical question about the possibility of knowledge?

A: On first glance, Plato seems to say that knowledge (truth) is *possible*, and that we arrive at it by means of *argumentative dialogue*. Nearly all of his writings are, in fact, in the form of dialogues. Nearly all of these so-called Socratic dialogues (named after Plato's teacher, Socrates, who always takes one of the roles) have a similar structure. They begin with a question, and attempt to find an answer – that is, the truth which has been sought.

The typical Socratic (more correctly, Platonic) dialogue comprises the following steps:

1. Socrates poses a question to his interlocutor (e.g. “What is justice?”).
2. The interlocutor responds with his opinion (Greek: *doxa*).
3. Socrates examines this opinion critically, tests its tenability, uncovers ambiguities or contradictions, and thus brings his interlocutor to:
4. Revise his original opinion and admit that it is untenable, thus bringing about a state of disorientation (Greek: *aporia*, “waylessness”).
5. Now the two partners in dialogue begin to search together for a way, for a possibly tenable answer. They weigh reasons and counter-reasons that speak for or against any proposed answers. A shared, argumentative search begins.
6. If the deliberation is successful (which it is not in every case), then the interlocutors will finally arrive at a consensus, which is supported by the arguments they have tested.

A proposition can be called “true” if the participants in the dialogue have arrived at a consensus (this can be called “consensual truth”). It is not the *fact* of consensus that matters but rather that the consensus is arrived at by deliberation. Yet, the newly found truth is always open to revision. When further arguments are brought up that place the hitherto accepted consensus in doubt, then the dialogue is re-opened. The renewed discussion may then prove either that the previous answer was untenable or that it has to be modified or that it was correct. In no case does the openness to revision devalue the claim to truth; quite the contrary, revision takes place in the name of truth.

Openness to revision distinguishes philosophical truth from dogmatic “truths” (of religion or ideology). This openness is inherently universalistic, for *every* argument can contribute to the discovery of truth. The limitation of the participants to certain groups is inadmissible, since that would contradict the purpose of the dialogue.

Q: And what does Plato’s answer reveal when we take a second look?

A: When we take the structure of Plato’s dialogues to be his answer to the fundamental philosophical question, we may well think: Yes, this is indeed the right answer – here and there we might elaborate or clarify, but in principle, this is it! Basically, the history of philosophy might appear to have ended before it even got started. Perhaps this is why the English philosopher Alfred North Whitehead remarked that the whole of the history of philosophy is nothing more than a commentary on Plato.

But this would be a premature judgment, since Plato himself, in the end, does *not* see dialogue as the tool that the *autonomous* human being needs in order to actively work towards the knowledge of truth. That a human as a rational being is necessarily autonomous was not comprehended until over 2000 years later, in the so-called Transcendental Philosophy of Kant. In Plato's view, dialogue is merely a tool which the human being can make use of to reassure himself of the truths he has already viewed before birth in the "world of ideas" (the Greek word *theorein* means to view, to contemplate). This "world of ideas" is the world of eternally valid truths, existing *independently* of the human being.

With this, Plato transforms man into an epistemologically heteronomous being; the autonomy of the Socratic dialogue is revoked by Plato's speculation about the world of ideas.

For Plato, the dialogue does not really construct truth. Since the truths viewed before birth are in any case present in every individual, the dialogue is no more than a means of helping the individual to rediscover them.

Q: What role does *Aristotle* play, seen against the background of Plato's dialogue-philosophy?

A: If the truth is worked out (or rediscovered) by means of the argumentative dialogue, then we must ask what such an argumentative dialogue really is – more specifically, what an argument really is. At what point do statements become arguments? When and how can we make inferences from one statement to another? These questions present themselves even when we accept, as Plato suggests at the "second level" of his epistemology, that dialogue is not the final instance in the search for truth but only a means to bring truth, originally perceived before birth, back into consciousness. Aristotle responded to this desideratum, which arose from Plato's dialogue philosophy, with the development of his "argumentation theory", later referred to as Aristotelian logic.

Q: Both Plato and Aristotle devoted much attention to questions of political philosophy, especially to the question: What should a good state look like? Is there a connection between the epistemological concepts of Plato and Aristotle and their respective political theories?

A: Indeed there is in both cases a clear connection between epistemology and political theory. For Plato – at the "second level" of his epistemology – truth exists independently of us, in the unfathomable, eternal "world of ideas". The conception of the "good state" is also such a truth; its form is eternally fixed, and is described in Plato's "Republic": the state is comprised of a productive, a protective and a governing class, who, like the members of the protective class, are forbidden to have private property, wives or children of their own. However, unlike the members of the other two classes, those in the governing class should have a higher insight into what is morally 'good' – they shall be "philosopher kings".

For the propagation of the two upper classes, there are exact rules of breeding. Children from unsanctioned relations must be killed.

Plato did not restrict this political philosophy to his own writings; he attempted to convince the rulers of small Greek city-states to implement his ideas.

It is irrelevant, based on Plato's idealist epistemology, whether such a state might in fact already exist in our world. Plato's state originates in the world of ideas – it has no localization in the empirically existing, quotidian world that we experience; it is, in Greek, *u-topian* (*u*meaning "without",*topos* meaning "place"). Its realization may require a complete reordering of the existing state. In this sense, Plato's political theory is *revolutionary* (*revolutio* meaning "turn over"). However, once the ideal state is realized, the problems of political community are solved once and for all. In this sense, Plato's concept of the state is *messianic*; that is, it holds the promise of redemption and, once realized, it is beyond criticism in every respect, and thus *totalitarian.* And since at this point there is nothing further to criticize or change, it is at the same time *ultra-conservative*. Moreover, as we have seen in his proposal for dealing with undesirably bred children, it is potentially prone to *violence*.

Aristotle never expressed himself explicitly with regard to his teacher's (Plato's) epistemology and political theory. In his writings, however, he presents a very different position. As already indicated, he developed in detail a theory of argumentation as an instrument for finding truth (in the group of writings known as "The Organon", or "Instrument").

By centralizing argumentation and leaving aside the connection to an independent, eternal and ideal realm of truth, it is not surprising that he arrived at a political theory essentially different from that of Plato.

Aristotle derives his conception of the state not from the "world of ideas" beyond us; rather, he surveys the historically given reality around him to see what kinds of states exist and what their relative advantages and defects are. His approach is thus not utopian in the manner of Plato, but *empirical*. And it is *eclectic* – the positive aspects identified shall be adopted when possible, and from the evident defects lessons shall be learnt in order to avoid them in the future. We must always attempt to see what "goes wrong", which dangers accumulate, and be prepared to react. We need to seek "solutions" to concrete problems; there is no notion of a final "redemption". We must strive towards *reform*, not messianic revolution.

For this reason, some believe that Aristotle should be considered conservative. This view misses the point, however – at least when the quality, extent and depth of the reforms have a profound impact. In such a case, a state may very well be so far "reformed" in a short period of time that we would not be able to recognize it afterwards.

It should be noted, by the way, that neither Plato nor Aristotle found any need in their ethics or political theory even to mention slavery, a common practice during their times.

Q: To what extent did these contrasting political theories influence the later development of political thought in Europe?

A: They had a formative influence, since, from a systematic point of view, these archetypal standpoints characterize the two positions that can be taken. The political theories of later periods, up to and including our own, can be situated within this polarity.

Q: To a detached observer, the dichotomy of *revolution* and *reform* might appear rather artificial. Is it really only revolution *or* reform?

A: No, as already suggested above. A *revolution* in the sense of a complete overturning of *all* circumstances of life is impossible in any case. Where would the "total revolutionaries" find the paper for their pamphlets, in what language would they write them, indeed, what clothes would they wear, what would they eat for lunch – if *each and every* aspect of the past were to be rejected? This would be absurd; a totally new beginning in this sense is impossible. But if we cannot achieve total revolution, we can at least achieve *partial* change. Let us say that the steel industry was nationalized (or privatized) yesterday – the bus would still pick us up at 6:45 to take us to work as normal. Even the most radical changes in one part of society can leave others entirely unchanged. "Well then, until after the war, at six," said Švejk, in the novel by Jaroslav Hašek, as he took leave of his drinking buddies – though that might have turned out differently to how Švejk imagined. When the comic Werner Fink, in an unforgettable cabaret sketch, returns as an emaciated foot soldier to the Wehrmacht office of a bombed-out German city in the early May of 1945 to "report for further duty", he finds an official sitting at his writing desk, covered with dust and mortar. And when the official, after wiping the dust out of his cuffs, says dryly, "The matter is closed", we know, terrible as it may seem, that a world may have collapsed, but life goes on, laconic and trivial (and we're unsure whether we should really laugh about it).

So, if it is not total *revolution* that is possible, but rather partial *reforms* - which can possibly have large-scale and far-reaching results – we must nevertheless keep in mind that, independent of their size, these reforms can only make sense when one knows to what *end* they are directed, and why *this* end in particular. Even when they are but small steps, they will still lead us somewhere and one should know if one wants to go where they lead and why.

Q: What is *Christianity's* answer to the fundamental philosophical question: How is truth possible – how can we find secure orientation?

A: Through the one transcendent God.

The previously made criticisms of Christianity qua religion do not need to be repeated here. All the same, from the perspective of philosophy, the monotheism of Christianity can be considered as eminent a progress as its ethics of neighborly love.

The One God is conceived as the God of *all* human beings; all are equal before Him, whether poor or rich, man or woman, young or old, Eskimo or Chinese. Christianity is universalistic, as is Greek philosophy. As does philosophy, Christianity raises a claim to truth. Making a serious claim to truth, however, means to make it with respect to *everyone*. The progress made by Christianity lies in the fact that it succeeded in adapting the universalistic claim, theoretically articulated in Greek philosophy, to practical life (at least in symbolic and ritualized forms). It was able to establish itself as a *way of life* – shaping a highly differentiated ecclesiastic life and integrating it into large sections of society, establishing a daily, yearly and life-long time-structure for its believers, and also carrying out extremely expansionist missionary activities (as a consequence of its claim to universal truth). It is not for nothing that "catholic" means "all-embracing".

It would be incorrect to ascribe this success entirely to the effects of external political forces or to the terror that the Church exerted once its power was established. Human beings, in the end, cannot be morally convinced by external power and terror, these forces are morally counter-productive. The core doctrine of Christianity that convinces and converts the hearts of people is the teaching of neighborly love: We are all equal before God and we are called upon by him to love one another.

Greek philosophy also taught that we are all equal (as rational, argumentative beings), and that we have no choice but to help one another in the search for truth. But philosophy's notions of equality and solidarity could, at best, only win over small groups within the educated classes of antiquity. It never managed to transform these ideas into a way of life. This was achieved, albeit only partially, by the second, the modern period of Enlightenment with its struggle for a democratic state of law and for institutions of social solidarity.

One thing must not be forgotten: Christianity's universalism and its principle of solidarity are grounded in *religion*. The instructions of universal neighborly love, which all people are bound to follow, come from *God*. The religious foundation of these progressive teachings is effectively the price that Christianity paid to spread them among humanity.

Europe was not yet ready to abandon the comfortable security of religion and enter the unguided autonomy of a mature existence. Evidently it needed further cultural development that would last many centuries.

In yet another respect, Christianity has contributed to progress in the cultural development of mankind, namely by removing God from the world in which we live, which, in Christianity, is called *this* world, as opposed to the *other* world, or the beyond. God is now located in the beyond; that is where he "exists", not in *this* world. This world is no longer full of gods, demigods, and daemons, fighting each other with lightning, storms, earthquakes, and so on. There is but one God, and He is in the beyond. Thus this world tends to be left on its own; it becomes mere *physis,* a "nature" which has to be accepted as it is. Only now does it make sense to search for the regularities which govern it. As long as the natural phenomena were thought of as playthings of the gods, this made no sense.

Only after the removal of God from this world did scientific exploration of nature become possible.

The groundwork for this is laid by Christianity, but at the same time it is forced to maintain some sort of connection between this world and the other: If God were to be entirely removed from this world, how could we then orient ourselves? We could only draw on our own resources, on our autonomous reason. But humanity was not yet ready for this insight (and it may still not be today).

Christianity has tried to solve this dilemma – namely, the need to pull the transcendent God back into our world in order to guide our profane lives – by creating a variety of *bridges*: the advent of Christ as God's son; the book in which the Word of God can be read; proofs of His existence; the idea of miracles through which God interferes into natural laws; the Church as a medium between man and God; the Pope as *Pontifex* ("bridge builder"); and so on.

In this way, the separation of the two worlds is only half-hearted. Yet, to be able to work, the natural sciences require a complete removal of God from nature. This move was only suggested by Christianity; it was carried out during Enlightenment. "Nature", as understood by the sciences, is everything that can be explored and studied in repeatable experiments by looking for regularly occurring changes, regularities that we then call "laws" (a somewhat unfortunate term insofar as it insinuates that nature "follows" these laws – in other words, that the laws have some sort of prior existence). In reality, however, the natural sciences can do nothing more than take note of regularities. Why these are as they are is something that science cannot explain. That natural regularities can at all be misunderstood in *this* sense (as if they could explain *why* they occur) may still be a consequence of Christianity's half-hearted removal of God from nature.

Q: What does Christianity's answer (to the fundamental philosophical question about the possibility of truth) mean for its conception of the state?

A: Above all that the state is subject to a higher (divine) power. The power of the state is not justified on its own terms, but must rather justify itself to a higher ethical instance, that of God. Thus domination is only legitimate to the extent that it derives from a divine assignment and subordinates itself to God.

The history of mankind is understood as an ongoing, never ending attempt to comply with God's will. Final redemption can only be attained in the other world, in what St. Augustine called *Civitas Dei* – the "City of God". The application of this basic concept in politics depends of course on the interpretation of God's will – the prerogative of the Church as God's representative on earth. It is self-evident that this allows for arbitrary machinations, especially when the interests of the Church are involved.

In the end, however, we can observe the following theoretical achievements: the supremacy of morality over politics, the universalistic claim of morality and the teleological sense of human history.

Q: What is the answer of the *Renaissance* to the fundamental philosophical question about the possibility of truth?

A: To sum up the centuries during which ancient philosophy was reborn after more than a thousand years of Christian domination is no simple endeavor – they are too multi-faceted and contradictory. We can, however, define two of its basic characteristics: (a) a turn away from the Christian world view which put God at its center, and (b) a new appreciation of man himself – his admirable strength, his abilities and high-flying ambitions. The human world is no longer a vale of tears from which only God can redeem us at the end of history. It is a place where man can try out his abilities, where he can flex his muscles.

However, the term "Renaissance" ("rebirth") is misleading, since an essential aspect of ancient philosophy (at least of that of Plato and Aristotle) was *not* reborn, namely the view of man as an essentially moral being. When asked the question "Who are you?" or demanded to "know himself", this man could only reply: "I can know myself only as a human among humankind; even the construction of my own identity requires the cooperation of other human beings; in recognizing myself, I must unavoidably recognize universal rules of coexistent life". Yet the moral-philosophical traditions of antiquity and the moral teachings of Christianity were not completely extinguished. They continued to exist, but were mixed with new viewpoints and attitudes that, strictly speaking, were incompatible with them.

Even in the writings of Machiavelli, perhaps the most salient representative of this new world, morality has not disappeared entirely. In “Il Principe” ("The Prince”), which lays out maxims and principles for the education of rulers, he invokes the moral good. But only in a marginal way. The core of his teaching is: The ruler may do anything; he may lie, intrigue, betray, bribe or murder when necessary to maintain and expand his power.

Q: Is that not a low point in the spiritual development of humanity? How was it reached?

A: To understand this development, we have to remember that, in Machiavelli’s time, the once mighty Roman Empire was all but dissolved. The Roman Empire saw itself as a world empire which upheld the rule of law among men. With its advancing dissolution, the authority that had been perceived as the protector of moral principles (embodied in its system of justice) was disappearing.

In its place something new had appeared: the modern state. The Roman state was not just *a* state in this sense – it claimed to provide the legal framework for all of humanity.

Now this *one* state was gradually replaced by an increasing number of individual states, each of which claimed sovereignty, that is, the right to regulate their internal and external affairs.

Prior to the rise of the Roman Empire, we also find individual states (like the Greek city-states). But at that time there was no understanding of universal justice, as would later be embodied in the Roman Empire.

With the establishment of Christianity as its state religion, the universalistic claim of Roman law was theologically and morally enhanced.

Accordingly, the fall of the Empire lead to the collapse of the universalistic morality it had previously embodied.

With the emergence of a multitude of states came the problem of conceiving, establishing and enforcing principles of justice *between* states, i.e. some kind of international law. Under the prevailing conditions, this problem could not be solved: the conceptual tools required were still lacking.

Machiavelli’s answer is thus: as a last resort, states resolve their conflicts through war. The right of the strongest (or most cunning, most vicious, most bloodthirsty) prevails.

States have done exactly this, including throughout two world wars – and often with enthusiasm.

The invention of weapons of mass destruction means that this simply cannot be continued. An aggressor might never recover, however convinced of his right to attack.

Kant presented an alternative. He called it the "Völkerbund" – a federation of states, based on voluntary subjection to the ultimate authority of a higher legal entity. More about this later.

Q: What role does *Protestantism* play in this context?

A: It paves the way for a further cultural and political weakening of the traditional universalistic authorities, both Catholic Church and Empire.

For Luther, the individual's relationship to God is not dependent on the Church. An individual can come to God simply by reading His Word. To this end, Luther translated the Bible into German. To the degree that individuals themselves are able to come to God in this way, the Church becomes obsolete; its raison d'être is undermined. In earlier times, the Church had met such attacks successfully by re-indoctrination, repression, and, when necessary, by physically wiping out the so-called heretics. Now, because of the newly arisen, uncertain relations of power (due to the gradual emergence of sovereign states), this was no longer possible. Nevertheless, in a war lasting thirty years, the Catholic powers tried to overcome the Protestant side, and in doing so laid waste to a large part of Germany, obliterating around a third of the population.

The decline of the universalistic authorities (Church and Empire) favored the position of the new rulers of the sovereign states. They now took on the role of "Defenders of the Faith", to the extreme of the principle "*cuius regio eius religio*" ("Whose realm, his religion"), thus raising the arbitrary right of the ruler and absolute domination of his subjects to a principle of the state.

As progressive as Luther's recourse to the insight of the individual may appear, it leads to a subjectivity by which the individual interpretation of a believer (Luther: "Here I stand; I can do no other") or the arbitrary power-oriented will of the territorial and religious ruler is enshrined as a sacrosanct guiding principle.

Q: Is the war of all against all really the last word?

A: No, it is only the lowest point of moral development – the transitory, apparent victory of man's animal instinct.

Q: But after the old, religiously grounded, universalistic authorities have lost their power, what could replace them?

A: The ideas of the Enlightenment; the autonomous reason of the human being, which develops over time. The catastrophe of the Thirty Years War and the revolutionary innovation with which it ended (i.e. the birth and recognition of sovereign states in the Peace of Westphalia), brought about the need for a new foundation, a new conception of how these sovereign states could coexist. The Catholic Emperor and the Catholic Church could no longer play this role. The sovereign states themselves had to define their relations to one another. But how? Two different answers have been given. One by Hobbes, another one by Kant.

Q: What is Hobbes's way out of the war of everyone against everyone?

A: For Hobbes, man is in fact nothing but an animal: "*Homo homini lupus*" ("Man is wolf to man"), he says. These wolves, in order to prevent themselves from ripping each other apart (i.e. out of self-interest), make a contract in which they agree, in case of conflict, to submit themselves to the power of a yet stronger beast, the so-called Leviathan (the state) – endowed by the wolves with the power to enforce its will.

Q: Is Hobbes's concept better than that of Machiavelli?

A: If Machiavelli's political theory represents the moral rock bottom, then things can in fact only get better. A Leviathan-state would indeed be better than the madhouse, or rather slaughterhouse, that results when we give the wolf-men free reign, as Machiavelli would have it.

Q: Can we see Hobbes's concept as a satisfactory model for the construction of the state?

A: No. At first glance, Hobbes's concept may seem convincing. It appears to offer a *moral-free* foundation for the construction of the state. From Hobbes's point of view, this must be the case since he sees human beings as nothing but animals. Yet upon closer examination, it becomes evident that Hobbes's theory is not moral-free, for it assumes that the wolves accept their contract as binding and do not slyly seek their own advantage to the detriment of others if they are sure that they will not be detected. It presupposes that the wolves have a moral duty to adhere to contracts.

Moreover, linguistic interactions such as the process of discussion which is necessary to reach an agreement (the basis of the contract), the wording of the contract itself and the communicative acts that necessarily follow thereafter (concerning, for example, its correct observance, the choice of sanctions for those who break it etc.) require mutually binding rights and duties to be recognized – a presupposition we cannot make with regard to wolves.

To what extent Kant's concept represents an advancement in the development of reason shall be discussed later on. At this point, this much can be said: Kant did not perceive man as an animal but as a being endowed with reason and the capacity for moral judgment.

Q: What is the answer of the *Enlightenment* to the fundamental philosophical question (about the possibility of truth)?

A: Here we have to distinguish between the empiricist Enlightenment and the Kantian Enlightenment.

The answer of the empiricist Enlightenment was that the senses given to all men by nature make reliable orientation possible. They show us "what is the case", what the world around us looks like.

They also enable us to find out what we should do and what we should not do. For this purpose, we have a special "moral sense" (Hutcheson), located in the "pineal gland" of the brain. This pineal gland produces pleasant feelings when we do the right thing and unpleasant ones when we do the opposite. The name "Empiricism" derives from the idea that *sensual experience* ("*empiria*") is considered to be the basis of knowledge.

This basis is universalistic because nature has endowed all human beings with the same sensory apparatus for gaining experiences.

Thus, from the standpoint of Empiricism, all human beings are equal (inspired by the empiricist Enlightenment, the United States Constitution states that "All men are born free and equal"), and they are able to find truth without divine instruction.

Q: Is there anything wrong with this?

A: In fact, yes. All men are free and equal, but not "by nature". They are free and equal only insofar as they understand that even in the simplest attempt to obtain knowledge/truth they have to *presuppose* themselves and their fellow men as free and equal.

Q: But surely no one can deny that we have natural senses, with which we can orient ourselves?

A: On the contrary, we cannot orient ourselves with the bare impressions we receive from our senses; we have to process them mentally and understand them *as information* about things that stand in spatial, temporal and causal relationships to one another. To this end, quite elaborate processes of interpretation may be necessary. The natural senses only provide us with the material from which the human mind can construct knowledge.

Q: Then it is *not* really correct to say that Empiricism sees man as a being that is able to find its way entirely on its own?

A: In the eyes of Empiricism, man is a part of nature. However, Empiricism claims to discover something objectively in its concept of nature which it has already tacitly placed there. Just as religion sees God as the source of knowledge, so too does Empiricism see nature. In both cases, a source of orientation *independent* of man is assumed. It is from this source that man *receives* his orientation. Like religion, Empiricism is epistemologically and ethically*heteronomous*.

Q: This is perhaps especially evident in the case of the "moral sense"?

A: The naïveté of this assumption is obvious. Experience teaches us that people often commit the most heinous crimes in perfect peace of mind, or even with joy and enthusiasm.

Unfortunately there is no such "moral sense" given to us by nature.

By nature we are neither good nor evil. "Nature" is not a moral concept. Nature is what it is, and no more. It does not take part in our fate, just as we cannot change it. We can use certain parts of nature for our good or evil purposes, but we cannot change nature *as such*. Even if we were to succeed in blowing up the world, we would only have succeeded because we had managed to understand how nature works, i.e., what natural processes we needed to bring about the explosion. But nature functions only as it functions. We can find out *how* nature functions, but we don't know *why* this is the case, e.g. *why* splitting the atom releases energy, *why* chemical reactions cause sugar to dissolve in coffee. In any case, if our planet were to disappear from the universe with its however many trillions of solar systems, it would be an insignificant event – at least, we know of no beings besides ourselves for whom it could have any "meaning".

Q: It may well be that there is no "moral sense". Sometimes, though, we have a bad feeling when we plan something, but at the same time think that it would really be better not to do it.

A: In that case it is probably our conscience that makes us uncomfortable. But conscience is not a "moral *sense*" because it is not given to us by nature. Rather, it is a set of moral attitudes, acquired through education and socialization, which allow us to make spontaneous judgments in case we have to act immediately. When we see an old man crossing the street just as a truck is suddenly closing in on him, we spontaneously reach to pull him out of danger. There is no time for ethical deliberation on the pros and cons of the action. We have to act quickly. This is possible only because we have acquired the ability to call upon those moral attitudes which we have adopted as habits. The presence (or absence) of these attitudes and the forms that they take (or fail to take) are the results of human learning processes.

It may be the case that we, like some animal species, have an instinctual inhibition against killing members of our own species when we see them face to face. We may well doubt, however, that such an inhibition truly exists, given that many homicides and murders occur in precisely this situation. Even if we accept its existence, it can at most be considered as *quasi*-moral, as moral-*analogue*, not as*moral* in a stricter sense of the word, precisely because it is *natural* and does not arise from insight.

Q: What is special about *Kant* and how does his answer differ from that of the empiricist Enlightenment?

A: Kant's outstanding contribution to the history of philosophy is the step from heteronomy to *autonomy*. We are no longer guided by the eternal truths of Plato which exist independently of humans, or by the timeless God of Christianity who exists independently of humans, or by the Empiricists' equally timeless and eternal natural world (existing independently of humans) that guides us. For Kant, man is autonomous; there is no external guide. Outside his own self there is no authority to which he could turn for orientation. He is left to his own devices; only he himself can find and judge the proper direction for his life, the criteria for true and false, good and bad.

Q: What motivates Kant to conceive of man as being autonomous? And what, according to Kant, can protect him from error? In other words: what compels us to accept that we must work out, for ourselves, what the world is (find out what *is* the case) and what we *should do* in it? What protects us from error?

A: Regarding the first part of this question (about autonomy), Kant gives a convincing answer; regarding the second (about protection from error) he does not. That answer will only be given later, by the philosophy of language of our time.

Kant's answer to the first part of the question is this: we cannot avoid reflecting on the conditions of the possibility of knowledge. Through this process of self-contemplation (which he calls transcendental reflection), we are forced to think of ourselves as autonomous beings.

(What Kant means by "transcendental reflection" was sketched out in Part I.) We cannot get beyond our insight into the conditions of the possibility of knowledge; e.g. we cannot know anything about the "thing in itself" (the "Ding an sich"), and we cannot know why the world, life and reason exist. The world exists only insofar as we construct it for ourselves, making use of concepts that we have not inferred from it – for at the beginning, we do not yet know "the world", but rather have to build it out of ourselves by using reason. Substance, time, space and causality are such concepts. The autonomy of the human being lies in the fact that he can create these concepts and understand "the world" through them, making use of the data given to him by his natural senses.

The activity of reason and the data provided by the senses belong together in the process of achieving knowledge: "Concepts without experience are empty; experience without concepts is blind", says Kant.

This autonomous achievement *is* – whether the human being is conscious of it or not – the condition for the possibility of knowledge. "The world" would not "exist" if human reason could not generate the concepts through which the world must initially be constructed as "existent".

This is the Copernican Turn of epistemology – it is no longer the case that the world exists, waiting to be perceived by us. Rather, the world "exists" insofar as we perceive it. "Existence" is a concept generated by human reason, something that does not occur in the outside world. "Until now, it was assumed that our knowledge must be oriented to objects. [...] Let us attempt [...] for once to see if we would not make more progress in the tasks of metaphysics by assuming that the objects have to orient themselves to our modes of understanding". These famous, provocative sentences in Kant's *Critique of Pure Reason* (Second Edition, XVI) should, of course, not be (mis)understood as saying that the world would cease to exist if humankind should cease to exist. Kant merely points out (though certainly with provocative exaggeration which invites misunderstanding) that, whether or not the world exists for *us* is dependent on our perception of it.

Q: To what extent is the transcendental epistemology of Kant, as indicated above, inadequate?

A: For Kant it is the solitary activity of the individual's reason which produces knowledge.

He did not yet see that the attainment of knowledge by human beings (for example, the creation of the concepts necessary to construct our world) always takes place in the medium of language; that it always implies language, communication and learning with and from other individuals.

Certainly, there are passages where Kant alludes to the communicative character of knowledge and its dependence on language. But such observations remain peripheral; language has no genuinely systematic role in Kant's epistemology. Knowledge, for Kant, is the product of the subject's individual reason; the co-subject (the fellow human being) is not involved, at least not as a *necessary* participant in the process.

This further development has only occurred in the philosophy of language of our time. To begin with, however, Kant's transcendental subjectivism provided German Idealist philosophers such as Fichte and Schelling with the basis for their Ich-philosophy. Even Husserl's solipsistic phenomenology and Heidegger's subjectivist conception of the "clearing" ("Lichtung") through which "Being emerges" can still only be understood against the background of the dialogical deficit of Kantian epistemology.

Q: How does Kant succeed in reaching a formal *universalist* ethics from a *subject*-oriented epistemology?

A: He does not succeed! Just as he fails to construct through dialogue what he calls the "fact of reason", simply positing it as something inherent in the individual, so too are the terms "you" and "we", used in the categorical imperative [1] (his highest moral principle), simply *posited*, as if they arose from the operations of reason within the isolated subject. This would be true only if Kant had seen, right from the start, the transcendental necessity of incorporating the co-subject (the "you" and "we") into the process of attaining knowledge. (These terms are needed even to ask the most simple question.)

Q: Can Kant's ethics be applied in practice? What about the critique of his moral rigorism?

A: For Kant, ethical maxims should be applied unconditionally (categorically). The maxim "Don't tell lies!" is valid at all times, without exception – even when, by telling the truth, we might deliver an innocent man who is being persecuted unjustly to his death. The consequences are irrelevant.

The only "good" is good will, expressed in a maxim. For Kant, maxims arise from purely theoretical operations of thought, carried out by the individual. If the world should be destroyed as a consequence of following such maxims, then so be it; it is our *duty* to follow them. In the end, this means: "*Fiat justitia, pereat mundus*". "Justice be done, even if the world shall perish".

This may appear abstruse, and one might at once object that an ethics which accepts that the world could be destroyed as a result of its own maxims would be self-contradictory, since it radically prevents the reasoned human being from achieving self-realization. Ethics should make our world better; if it leads to the world's destruction, it misunderstands itself.

In our time, we have no cause to dismiss Kant's position smugly. Not so long ago, in the days of the cold war, the slogan "Better dead than red" was propagated even by prominent philosophers. This slogan follows the argumentative patterns of Kantian maxim rigorism.

Q: Why did Kant insist on this position?

A: If he had not understood his ethics in purely categorical terms (in other words, if he had recognized that conditions exist under which exceptions

---

1 "Act only according to that maxim whereby you can, at the same time, will that it should become a universal law", that is, so that we *all* can adopt it!

from an otherwise morally good rule, such as "Don't tell lies!", can be justified), he would have had to give up his subjectivist foundation. However, he did not have an alternative foundation based on dialogue. He would have needed to abandon his categorical approach, because exceptions are unforeseeable (not calculable). They arise in the unpredictable course of history. As justifiable exceptions, they can be invoked only by those living at the time.

Q: If exceptions arising out of a specific situation are admitted, how can we prevent ethics from, so to speak, drowning in a sea of exceptions? In other words, how do we justify, or not justify, exceptions?

A: This is certainly *the* crucial question in the implementation of ethics. The theoretical solution lies in what Kant calls the "faculty of judgment" ("Urteilskraft"), which allows the human being to assess the specific conditions under which he must act in a given situation at a given moment. For example, if I know where the innocent man is hiding I will have to decide whether I should lie to his persecutors or tell them the truth. For this purpose I need to judge whether the persecutors would in fact kill the man, or whether the pursuit might merely end with a heated argument and an eventual resolution of the misunderstanding. Only those who are in this situation and have to react immediately are capable of forming a sound judgment.

An alternative "application of the faculty of judgment" that might get around Kant's moral rigorism could consist of the following steps:

- Identification of the ethical maxims which are in conflict,
- Prognosis of what would happen if each maxim were followed,
- Decision for one of the expected outcomes, based on a
- Justification of this decision referring to a "mediating" maxim, which shows that our decision leads us closer to more human living conditions – i.e. conditions which best allow man to realize himself as a rational being.

In the case described above, this could mean: I lie to the persecutors, saving the life of the man. Then I bring both sides to trial: the persecutors for attempted murder and the persecuted man for the deed for which he was being persecuted. My "mediating" maxim might then be formulated as:

"Make an exception to the maxim to tell the truth when lying would prevent a disaster and at the same time preserve the possibility of resolving the conflict within the norms of justice".

In this case there can be no doubt that a trial, which allows the accused to defend themselves, is a more rational solution for human beings than a vengeful murder brought about by telling the truth.

Q: That may be fine in theory, but does it work in practice?

A: The deliberations described above of course require the individual to have the will and the ability to carry them out. In practice, both are often lacking. Otherwise, we would be living in a better world. However our world is not simply a "hell on earth". Within history we can also see the gradual unfolding of human reason and together with that the development of the "faculty of judgment" in everyday life.

Q: What is the political-philosophical answer of Kant (in contrast to Hobbes) to the gradual dissolution of traditional, religiously founded universalistic authorities?

A: They are replaced by an *enlightened public* within each state (including the relevant institutions) and a "League of Nations" between the states.

The raison d'être of the state is to secure the external conditions necessary for the unfolding of reason. Foremost among these are freedom of expression and the adherence to fixed rules (those of a system of justice) in the resolution of conflicts.

On an international level, the League of Nations has the same task: to ensure the freedom of expression of all member states, and to establish the rules of international law to resolve conflicts among them.

Q: How does this answer differ from that of Hobbes?

A: Kant sees war as the *natural* state of affairs. This he shares with Hobbes, who sees man as a wolf, as a part of nature.

Yet Hobbes's solution changes nothing in this respect. The wolves remain wolves, even after they have made the pact to form a state. They make the pact to prevent themselves from mauling each other, so that they may continue to live as wolves. Kant, however, seeks to overcome the state of nature. In contrast to Hobbes, he recognizes that man is *more* than a part of nature. When human beings resolve their conflicts through violence, they act like animals, just as occurs in nature. Man is not realized as a *human* being when he acts in this way; instead he turns himself into a beast.

For Kant, too, the state is founded on a contract. This contract, however, is possible only because man is *not* an animal; his moral insight is a condition upon which the contract is made.

Q: How does the *philosophy of history* answer the fundamental philosophical question about the possibility of knowledge (truth)?

A: Its very name suggests the answer: secure orientation is made possible by history, for history is where the gradual unfolding of reason takes place. We can learn what reason is by looking at history. "All that is real is rational," in the words of Hegel. The individual epochs of history are successive stages in the development of reason. And even if this often does not appear to be so, this is merely the "cunning of reason". For, from a greater distance, it can be seen that even suffering has a reasonable purpose, insofar as it gives people cause to learn from it.

Philosophy of history does not concern itself with the irreducible and inevitable nature of transcendental reflection – in which reason constitutes itself. Just as Plato believed that truth could be found in the "world of ideas", Christianity in a transcendent God, and Empiricism in a hypostatized nature, Hegel believed it could be found in history.

"Truth", however, cannot be found *outside* of man. It can only be "found" there because interpretation has brought it into existence. The world of ideas, God, nature and history have been conceived (by man) as places where reason can be found.

The philosophy of history deals with the problem of Kant's transcendental subjectivism insofar as it attempts to compensate for Kant's missing co-subject by replacing it with "history". In doing so, however, it misunderstands Kant's concept of *autonomous* reason and falls back to the stage of pre-Kantian heteronomy.

Since, in contrast to the other pre-Kantian heteronomous philosophies, it postulates no *eternal* truths, but rather sees the continual change of history as the place of reason, it has no arguments which could prevent it from dissolving into precisely this history itself – its concept of reason sinks into a sea of relativistic historicism.

Seeing human history as the place in which reason can be discovered or better, in which reason constitutes itself (rather than in the world of ideas, in transcendence or in nature which are all lacking human beings) at least indicates that a co-subject is necessary for the constitution of reason.

However, rather than founding the concept of reason on transcendental dialogue from the beginning (in other words, on obtaining it via dialogic-transcendental reflection), the philosophy of history throws the baby out with the bathwater, by interpreting into history a concept of reason that it would have needed to construct for itself first.

Q: Did Marx save the philosophy of history by turning Hegel "from his head onto his feet"?

A: Marx did in fact attempt to fill out Hegel's interpretation of world history (as the gradual self-realization of world-reason) by giving it a materialistic foundation.

Q: How can we be sure, according to Marx, that this self-realization actually takes place?

A: We are assured of this because laws of economic and social development, which he understands as laws of nature, inevitably lead towards communism in which the domination of man by man is overcome. Only then can the human being realize himself through the free use of reason. In this sense, communism represents the end of history as we have known it, a history of class struggles (slaves vs. masters; nobility, clergy and guilds vs. peasants), where the relationship between the classes (as well as the emergence of new classes and the decline of others) depends on the development of the economic *means* of production (manual or mechanized production, automation, means of transport) and of the associated *relations* of production (the type of relationships between relevant socioeconomic groups).

The *means* of production of our time emerged in the English industrial revolution of the eighteenth and nineteenth century, which built on new discoveries in the natural sciences and on parallel technological developments. The *relations* of production are those of capitalism. Marx predicts that industrial capitalism, after a period of intensifying class struggles, leads to communism.

Q: Why does Marx see capitalism as leading to communism? Today it seems that capitalism is leading to even more capitalism!

A: It may look that way, but perhaps the last word has not yet been spoken. The core of capitalism is the creation of surplus value. Following the Italian-English economist David Ricardo, Marx recognized that human labor has the capacity to create surplus value. "Surplus value" is the difference between the value that must be invested in order to produce something (an object or a situation) and the value of the finished product. If, for example, a farmer spends three months cultivating a field and during this time must consume 150 kg of grain to sustain his work power, before finally harvesting 200 kg, his work will have created a "surplus value" of 200 – 150 = 50 kg. This becomes "capital" if it is reinvested for the purpose of creating further surplus value.

Under the conditions of science-based industrialism, this process has become highly efficient. In pre-industrial societies, the possibilities for creating surplus value were limited, since both the means of production and the relations of production were underdeveloped.

Large portions of the surplus value produced were diverted to non-economic ends, such as the construction of cathedrals or the luxury consumption of ruling classes. A blatant example of this is the uneconomic, pre-capitalist use (or, in capitalist terms, squandering) of the "surplus value" obtained by the Spanish crown and nobility in completely plundering several developed cultures of Central and South America. A prerequisite for the development of capitalism is, of course, a cultural disposition that recognizes the importance of increasing surplus value. Max Weber showed that this disposition could initially be found in the cultural milieu of northern Italy and in societies influenced by Lutheran and Calvinist Protestantism.

The repeated reinvestment of surplus value leads to the growth of the respective company. The more goods a company produces the less each one costs. In this way the company can gain an advantage over its competitors. The expansionism inherent in this system demands ever larger markets (ultimately the world market) and at the same time leads to a reduction in the number of companies, as the stronger ones drive out or swallow up the weaker ones. Following the logic of this development, the number of companies will ultimately be reduced to one. This tendency can be seen clearly when comparing the number of banks, automobile and aircraft companies, or chemical or feed producers, which were operational 40 years ago with the few that exist today.

This result is one of Marx's predictions: in capitalism the number of companies will shrink. He also predicts that the number (and the misery) of workers dependent on capital owners (whether persons or companies) will rise. The capital owners obtain their surplus value not by producing it themselves, but by having others, the so-called proletarians, work for them; however they give them as little of the surplus they created as possible, in order to increase their profit. The capital owners need to exploit the proletarians to the greatest extent they can.

The increasing misery of the proletarians caused by this necessity, in combination with their large and increasing numbers (and the small and decreasing number of capital owners) finally leads to a worldwide uprising of the proletariat – to the elimination of the capitalists as a class, and thereby to the end of class society, since only the working class remains. With this final step, the domination of man by man comes to an end.

Q: Didn't Marx fail to see that it is in the capitalist's interest to sell his products to his own workers, and that to do this, he must divert a larger share of his profits to them (increase of the domestic demand)?

A: This is true, and this interest has in fact led to an impressive increase in the general standard of living in the core countries of capitalism. Nevertheless, it is also true that the capital owner can increase his profit only to the extent that he gives less of it away.

When we turn our view away from these core capitalist countries to the world market, we would have to be blind not to see that the misery described by Marx (and not only by him, but also by observers from quite different political spectrums) persists on the *world* scale. Nowadays is not only a large part of humanity subject to exploitation but also the natural resources essential to its survival. Capitalistic exploitation certainly cannot be held solely responsible for world poverty and for the ongoing destruction of natural resources. The enormous growth in population, for example, is another important cause.

Whether this development of the globalized capitalistic economy will ultimately lead to the end of the capitalist class and thereby to the end of the domination of man by man, is certainly doubtful given the low level of enlightenment on the global scale. On the other hand, we may well hope that humanity's instinct for self-preservation will eventually counteract the self-destructive consequences of globalized capitalism, at least in the existentially most important areas (military technology and the destruction of non-renewable natural resources) and force society to accept the higher principle of the preservation of life – all the more so, since this principle lies in the well-understood long-term interests of the capitalist system itself.

As interesting and important for our times as Marx's analysis may be, it must be said, that, when we assess the answer his theory of history provides for our fundamental philosophical question about the possibility of knowledge, his reference to history is epistemologically misguided, since the concept of reason that Marx attempts to derive from economic history must have already existed beforehand. Yet the question about the origin of reason remains unanswered.

Q: Can we do away with capitalism?

A: The discovery of surplus value and the possibility of turning it into capital in order to generate yet more surplus value, is something that cannot be reversed – even if the means of production are nationalized or transformed into some other kind of common property. Even those societies which called themselves "socialist", such as the Soviet Union, were in fact capitalist: they created surplus value and reinvested it. Yet, those who directed the process were not private persons but rather state bureaucrats.

The Cold War which for decades threatened the very existence of mankind was not a conflict between capitalism and communism but rather between private and state capitalism.

In addition, in neither of these two systems did the respective model (private/state capitalism) exist in a pure form. Both were in reality mixed systems (private *and* state capitalism), with the private sector probably being much smaller in the "socialist" states than the public sector in the "capitalist" ones. The Soviet Union had a significant private agricultural subsistence economy with a corresponding retail trade; in Poland, the agricultural sector was mostly private; various countries of the "socialist camp" had private handicrafts and retail. In all of these countries the family structure was retained and households were private, as was early childhood education.

In the United States, which is seen by many (including itself) as the core country of modern capitalism, large parts of the economy are not in the hands of private persons, but rather belong to the federal government, the states or the municipalities (for example, parts of the healthcare, the road management, the public transport system and the postal service). On top of this is the very large military supply sector, which is privately owned but dependent on state funding. It is in this indirectly state-managed sector or in research centers financed and controlled by the state (such as NASA and the National Institutes of Health) that a large share of the nation's technical innovations take place. Moreover, the public sector is the largest employer in the country. This was true during the Cold War and has hardly changed despite all the neo-liberal and neo-conservative campaigns. An economic analysis of the European Union would certainly show that EU Institutions and the member states exert an even larger influence on economic life.

During his famous visit to West Germany, the General Secretary of the GDR, Erich Honecker, said that socialism and capitalism were like fire and water. His host, Chancellor Helmut Kohl, agreed. Both of them seriously believed that that was true. But it was pure ideology. By no means a harmless ideology, though – for several decades, it was used as the justification for an arms race beyond all comprehension, one that even led to the threat of "overkill", i.e. the technological ability to annihilate the enemy not once but several times over.

In the name of these obviously untenable ideologies, the world was turned into a madhouse.

While these two protagonists of the two supposedly irreconcilable systems were giving their speeches, their economic specialists might well have been busy negotiating and signing treaties on mutual cooperation, joint ventures, import-export business and so forth.

Even Lenin contracted capitalist companies to help with the electrification of the recently established Soviet Union. And today, the "communist" People's Republic of China has become one of the leading capitalist economic powers.

In short, the global capitalist economic order seems to be unchangeable; it is not bound to any particular system of ownership.

Which ownership mixture is best (e.g. private, central state, provincial, communal or cooperative ownership) cannot be determined without knowing the specific context. The ideologists of a pure state economy claimed to have a master plan that would deliver mankind from every evil. Similar promises are made by the ideologists of private capitalism, especially by the representatives of neo-liberalism. Both are wrong. Many aspects must be taken into consideration, from the purely technical and economic to the historical, cultural and political. And it is often the 'soft' aspects of culture and history that turn out to be the genuinely 'hard' determinants.

Q: For Marx, capitalism was the root of all evil and, accordingly, its end was to be the gate to paradise. But doesn't capitalism also have its good sides?

A: In the context of human history, the great achievement of capitalism is that, for the first time, it provides the possibility to overcome the traditional "economy of scarcity". The capitalist reinvestment of surplus value allows production to be increased to such an extent that it can satisfy not only the needs of 'normal' everyday life (such as food, clothing and shelter) but also the desire for luxury. This is particularly true under the given conditions of science- and technology-based industrialism. The core capitalist countries have indeed become "consumption" or even "affluent" societies – to a high degree at the costs of an ever more exploited and destroyed nature. This is a new development in the history of humanity.

Capitalism is thus not just unchangeable; it is a great achievement. However, it can only have this effect if its enormous inherent power is used to protect the structures of human society and is not allowed to destroy them. Simply put, we need a *political economy* that on the one hand encourages capitalism's ability to create surplus value (as is necessary for human progress), but, on the other hand, keeps its inherent tendency to exploit human labor and natural resources under control.

From a German perspective, this means: Article 14.2 of the Basic Law (the Constitution) must be fleshed out and brought to life.

Returning to our fundamental philosophical question about the possibility of knowledge (truth), we must conclude that the philosophy of history evidently also fails to give a satisfying answer. By understanding history as the vehicle in which reason constitutes itself, it fails to see that the very concept of reason needs to be constructed first, and that this endeavor, from the beginning, will have to incorporate the co-subject.

Q: What possibilities remain at this point?

A: *First*, we can put aside the co-subject and rely simply on the ingenious "Ich", the "Übermensch". The so-called Ich-philosophy of German Idealism (Fichte, Schelling) and, more radically, Nietzsche, represent this option.

Second, we can call off the search for a specifically philosophical answer, concern ourselves with those areas of life in which it appears that truth is really found, and then try to work out *how* it is found. Possible areas for this are the sciences and everyday knowledge. These are the objects of study of: analytical philosophy of science (Vienna Circle), critical rationalism (Karl Popper) and analytic philosophy of ordinary language (G. E. Moore).

Third, we can answer the question in the negative: there simply is*no* possibility – we must give up the claim for truth. This is the position taken by the "post-modernists" (Lyotard, Derrida, Foucault, Welsch, Feyerabend, Rorty).

And *fourth*, it appears to me that it might be worth a try to extract Kantian transcendentalism from its subjectivist orientation and make it workable by including the co-subject.

Q: Let's at least have a brief look at each of these positions!

First, the *Ich-philosophy* of German Idealism (Fichte, Schelling, Nietzsche): renouncing the co-subject, relying on the ingenious Ich, on the Übermensch – what about this?

A: The Ich-philosophy of German Idealism represents an attempt to transform Kant's subjective transcendentalism into a system that starts from the Ich and reaches out to cosmology; thus explaining the world solely on the basis of the Ich. This can only end in autistic flights of fancy or religious speculation. Nietzsche offers an 'escape' from this dead end: it consists in a desperate last effort to set all hope on that single individual who can lead us by virtue of his naturally endowed genius. Nietzsche's concept of genius is an amalgamation of the empiricist idea of nature (according to which the human being has been endowed from the beginning with certain cognitive abilities) and Kantian subjectivist transcendentalism. The genius is the Übermensch, superior to the normal human being, which also means that he is above normal human reason. He, so to speak, embodies the exception.

The genius hears "the rustle of God's mantle through history" (as Bismarck said).Because he carries godliness within him, he stands above our simple morals. Indeed, moral rules, such as the Christian ones, are objects of derision for him, silly human foibles that only hinder the unfolding of the Übermensch's genius.

With his arrogant rejection of common humanity, Nietzsche opens the way to idiocy (a word that originally means "privacy") – even in his own personal life.

It is obvious that the National Socialists could easily make use of this cult of genius for their own Führer cult. The idea of the "Ausnahmezustand" (state of exception) in Carl Schmitt's controversial theory of state law is also influenced by that. (cf. Carl Schmitt:"Die Diktatur", 1921; and "Politische Theologie", 1922.). Here the exception (which Kant's ethics categorically rejected) is permanently granted to the one who happens to be perceived as a genius.

In any case, with Hitler in mind, Kant's categorical rejection is understandable on a human level. The tragedy of the conservative Protestant resistance against Hitler in the military was that, with true Kantian rigor, they felt themselves bound by oath and unable to allow any exception.

Q: *Second*: *Analytical philosophy*: Science and everyday knowledge as empirically given sources of orientation. Wouldn't we find a solution (that is, an answer to the question about the possibility of knowledge) if we simply put the grand philosophical theories aside and paid attention to the obvious empirical fact that knowledge (truth) exists, and simply ask why this is so. Would that be the solution?

A: Indeed. One could well argue that, up to now, epistemology has not been able to demonstrate the possibility of knowledge systematically, yet it cannot be disputed that the enormous successes of science and technology would not exist if we could not obtain knowledge! The thing to do would simply be to analyze *how* knowledge is acquired; then we would have the answer we are looking for.

The same can be said for our everyday knowledge: no one can seriously dispute that we normally get along pretty well with our day to day affairs, which would not be possible if we did not have accurate information (knowledge). If we say to a salesperson, "May I have two currant buns, please", we will get them. This simple transaction presupposes knowledge on our side (we see the buns) and on the salesperson's side (who also sees the buns), as well as successful communication between both sides. Our daily life consists of a plethora of such processes. Against the background of these everyday experiences, the problems posed in epistemology must seem at least a little strange. Let's analyze exactly what we are doing when we order two buns; then we will know the answer to the question of how knowledge is possible!

Q: Isn't that plausible?

A: The analyses of how both scientific and everyday knowledge are brought about mark an important progress in the history of epistemology. Inspired by Kant, neither one attempts to find truth as a given fact (e.g. in the Platonic world of ideas, in Christian transcendence, in Empiricist nature, or in Hegelian history), but rather they understand truth as something we, as human beings, must construct and work on. To this end, they analyze the relevant scientific and everyday *processes*.

In this respect, analytical philosophy is on the right path, especially when it addresses everyday *language* and the *language* of science, given that, in both realms, the construction of knowledge takes place in the medium of language – or more generally, through communication.

Q: Does analytical philosophy provide a satisfactory answer to the fundamental philosophical question about the possibility of knowledge?

A: However much the achievements of analytical philosophy's detailed investigations into the methods of science, the language of science and everyday language are to be applauded [1] (and with them the insights made into the structures and interrelationships among the sciences as well as between them and the outside world), *analytical* philosophy, in the sense that it understands itself, is incompatible with the *normative*-ethical foundations of epistemology. If it were to incorporate these foundations, it would, in its own terms, cease to be scientific analysis and would descend to the level of unscientific partisanship of a practical, ethical or political nature.

---

1 A detailed discussion lies beyond the scope of this book, which is intended only to sketch the basic ideas and awaken interest in them.

Q: Weren't some members of the *Vienna Circle* of analytical philosophy socialists? Wasn't there a so-called "left wing" (Neurath, Carnap, Schlick)?

A: Those members of the Vienna Circle who were socialists were so out of personal conviction, not due to any philosophical or scientific reasons.
"Science" for the members of the Vienna Circle meant, above all, the natural sciences and mathematics. They intended to describe how these disciplines function internally. The only task of philosophy, then, was to determine whether scientific propositions are *logically* correct. Propositions that extended beyond the domain of the sciences were dismissed as "metaphysical". Rudolf Carnap even claimed that, from the logic of scientific propositions, one could deduce "the logical structure of the world". They saw no connection between science and practical life, particularly not in any sense that would have let science appear to be *dependent* on practical life.

Q: Doesn't this stance remind us of *Max Weber's* conception of science?

A: For his own field, sociology, Max Weber did in fact postulate a strict separation from practical life, especially from politics (even though he personally suffered from this separation). He saw practical life (the "Lebenswelt") as characterized by the "struggle of worldviews" ("Kampf der Weltanschauungen"). These stand in a direct, irreconcilable conflict. As a *scholar*, he could not comment on these conflicts –he could only do this as a human being and as a citizen with a particular "Weltanschauung". The struggle has to be carried out, the stronger side will win – such is the way of the world. Scholarly reason can analyze the struggle, but no more.
When we bear in mind the radical consequences of this "struggle of worldviews" in the Second World War (between Bolshevist and National-Socialist world-views) and later in the Cold War (between "democratic" and "totalitarian" world-views) its reach becomes clear, and some of us will ask what sciences and scholarship are for, if all they can say is that it would be interesting to write an analytical research project about this.

Q: But doesn't the *Critical Rationalism* of K. R. Popper claim to be not just an analysis of the methods of science but also a political program!

A: That is correct; however, Popper's conception of science cannot provide a sound basis for his political postulates.
For Popper, there is no positive notion of truth. There is only "trial and er-

ror". Just as nature brings forth a limitless variety of species, human efforts to find truth produce a limitless number of "hypotheses". Darwinian natural selection is paralleled by the scientific procedure of falsification. Falsification comprises two steps: firstly, we determine which of the (potentially unlimited number of) hypotheses are at all capable of being falsified, that is, which *can* be tested at all; the second step is then the carrying out of the respective tests. The hypothesis "Angels have wings" would, accordingly, be abandoned during the first step. "There is a bicycle lying on the moon", on the other hand, would remain, because we can in fact devise a way of testing whether or not it is true. It would probably not "survive" the second step. Popper regards the surviving hypotheses not as propositions whose "truth" has been proved, but merely as the ones which so far have survived all attempts at falsification.

These ideas of Popper had a worldwide resonance. It would not be wrong to see in his Critical Rationalism the West's philosophical answer to Marxism. This success is not surprising. There are two reasons for this, an explicitly declared one and a more hidden one.

The explicitly declared reason is that this conception of science requires an "open society", a society tolerant enough to allow any and all theories to be discussed, and all tests potentially capable of falsifying them to be carried out. This conception complies not only with the ideals of enlightenment, democracy and pluralism of western societies. An "open society" (one in which free discussion is permitted) is in and of itself desirable, and is a prerequisite for free interaction among people, quite independently of whether or not one accepts Popper's epistemology.

The other reason may be seen in the underlying, implicit justification of Darwinian style private capitalism in Western societies, as suggested by the comparison between Darwinian natural selection and scientific development: if even science functions in this way, then so much the better that the economic system does too!

Q: Why is Popper's theory of science philosophically untenable?

A: Because its fundamental thesis is self-contradictory. The assertion "There is no truth, only falsification" can only be understood as seriously meant if we read it as: "It is true: there is no truth, only falsification". One can also apply this argument to the notion of falsification, since falsification relies on an implicit acceptance of the notion of truth. We can only know what is false when we know what is true. For example, "It is true: the proposition that there is a bicycle on the moon is false".

Q: Setting the self-contradictory epistemological structure of Popper's theory aside, would his ideas nevertheless have social and political applications?

A: It has already been said that the concept of an "open society" is desirable. The concrete actions taking place within the "open society" would be what Popper called "piece-meal" projects: in accordance with Popper's epistemology, such projects would be started tentatively ("trial") and continued until they perhaps turn out to be an "error". It becomes clear that Popper's social technology program cannot be implemented when we consider a possible tentative project like "the replacement of all sources of energy with nuclear power": we would build nuclear power plants and then wait to see if any catastrophic disaster occurred. If this falsification were successful, we would then abandon the program.

Q: *Third*: *Post-modernism.* Can we give up the claim to truth altogether?

A: No. Strictly speaking, we humans cannot live without the claim to truth and without having found concrete truths. Someone who writes "I have no claim to truth" on the blackboard would overlook the fact that, in a trivial sense, he has already made use of quite a lot of truth just in order to write that sentence. He must have correctly identified the blackboard and the chalk as such, he has to choose the letters correctly, and he must have correctly ascertained that he has an audience.

In a moderate sense, the claim to truth is abandoned by post-modernism. It turns against the "Unitarian" (Eurocentric) notion of reason, to which it ascribes totalitarian tendencies. In reality, it says, there are not only various "reasons", but, beyond these, there are also other ways of comprehending the world. J.-F. Lyotard substituted, in this sense, what he called "meta-narrative" with many "small narratives", each of which has its own legitimacy.

A more radical stance is taken by Rorty who says that he asserts nothing in his own works (that he makes no claim to truth), but only narrates. With this we return to the pre-philosophical myths, which indeed only narrated and made no claim to truth.

Q: What should we think about that?

A: Epistemologically speaking, neither position would be worth considering (given the fact that they obviously cannot be sustained, as demonstrated above) if they did not have such a marked resonance.

However, how should we think of human beings who live in a world which – really and truly – is not lacking problems and who at the same time – really and truly – grant themselves the luxury of rejecting the very notions of reality and truth? This is evidently not an epistemological problem but rather a psychological and cultural one.

Q: *Fourth*: After all this, would it perhaps not be worth an effort to free Kantian *transcendental* philosophy from its subjectivism and make it fully functional, by taking into account the *co-subject* as an integral and necessary component of the process of gaining knowledge?

A: This question shall remain standing – not as an open question (the thoughts sketched in the first part of this book represent such an effort) but rather as a challenge to the reader to form his own critical (and self-critical) opinion, and take a position.

For how does the saying go? “Let your word be yes, yes; no, no”.

Historical Overview:

Answers to the question of how knowledge is possible

Myth:

The myth (narration) is an *un-conscious* answer.
It is philosophy which first asks the question *consciously*.

Plato:

Knowledge is gained in *argumentative dialogue (Socratic dialogue)*. But (for Plato) dialogue is only a means of revealing the eternal truths seen before birth in the *"realm of ideas"*. These exist independently of human beings (= heteronomous epistemology).

Aristotle:

Does not explicitly deny Plato's speculations about the realm of ideas. However, he develops a detailed theory of argumentation, later called Aristotelian logic.

Christianity:

Knowledge is attained by entering into a bond (*re-ligio* means "re-bind") with *God*. God is transcendent. There is but one God.

Renaissance:

Anthropocentric rather than theocentric.
Fundamental questions about knowledge become peripheral (including those about moral knowledge), since interest centers on human abilities.

EMPIRICISM:

Knowledge can be acquired through the *naturally* given senses, including a moral sense. All humans are equal as natural beings.

KANT:

Knowledge is made possible by the individual's autonomous use of reason.
Reflection on the conditions for the possibility of knowledge (=*transcendental reflection*) provides the basis for epistemology and ethics.
However: The co-subject is not made part of the process by which knowledge is attained.

PHILOSOPHY OF HISTORY:

Knowledge (reason) is constituted by *history*.
For Marx reason is first fully realized within communism, which is the first genuinely free form of society.
This is a necessary result of economic laws within history.

NIETZSCHE:

There is no interpersonal reason or morality.
Only the genius of the exceptional person, or Übermensch, can provide guidance.

ANALYTIC PHILOSOPHY:

Knowledge can be found by analyzing the methods of science and both scientific and everyday language.
However these analyses are by necessity not normative.

POSTMODERNISM:

There is not one single truth but many; additionally, there are other paths to reality besides (the various forms of) reason.
Rorty abandons the claim to truth altogether. Rather, he only wants to narrate, as did the myths.

TRANSCENDENTAL-PRAGMATIC THEORY OF KNOWLEDGE:

We cannot get beyond the claim to truth.
Every seriously posed question necessarily contains the reciprocal acknowledgement of rights and duties, and thus the acknowledgement of basic, virtually universalistic, ethical norms. Even those who contest this in theory would, in the very act of contesting, make use of it and thus unwittingly accept it in practice.

THE THREE MOST IMPORTANT STEPS (FROM A CRITICAL STANDPOINT):

1.) PLATO:

Along with his teacher Socrates he maintains that truth is found in argumentative dialogue. This would answer the fundamental philosophical question concerning the possibility of knowledge, had Plato not devalued it with his speculation about the realm of ideas, rendering argumentative dialogue merely a tool which enables us to re-discover the eternal truths seen before birth in the realm of ideas.

According to his theory, the human being itself does not construct truth (autonomously) through argumentative dialogue; rather, truth exists independently of the human being (= heteronomous concept of truth).

2.) KANT:

The step from heteronomy to autonomy. The human being itself constructs truth by using reason.

As in Plato, the possibility of finding truth exists for both questions about our knowledge of the world (theoretical reason) and for ethical questions (practical reason).

Kant corrects Plato's heteronomous epistemology and thus carries out the "Copernican turn" in the history of philosophy: the irreducible foundation of all knowledge is transcendental reflection, that is, reflection on the conditions for the possibility of knowledge.

We accept these conditions whenever we attempt to gain knowledge.

However, Kant overlooks the fact that the subject's efforts to attain knowledge always and necessarily involve the co-subject (thus, virtually all beings endowed with reason) as a constitutive part of these efforts (i.e. as a condition for the possibility of knowledge). In this sense he falls behind the dialogue-oriented philosophy of Socrates and Plato.

3.) Transcendental pragmatics:

The human being is autonomous. The claim to truth is ineluctable.

The effort to find knowledge is always dialogical (i.e. virtually universalistic); it always presupposes the participation of the co-subject.

The conditions for the possibility of knowledge inevitably imply the acknowledgement of (virtually universalistic) ethical norms.

Transcendental philosophy thus adopts Plato's philosophy of dialogue (in opposition to Kant's subjectivism), defends Kant's autonomy against Plato's heteronomy, and extends Kant's subjective transcendentalism to a dialogic transcendentalism that includes the co-subject.

Index of Names and Topics: